# BLACK CAKE, TURTLE SOUP, and other dilemmas

# BLACK CAKE, TURTLE SOUP,

### and other dilemmas

## GLORIA BLIZZARD

DUNDURN
PRESS

Excerpts from Selwyn Ryan, (2009) *Eric Williams: The Myth and the Man*. Page 652. Reproduced and distributed with the permission of The University of the West Indies Press, uwipress.com/9789766402075/eric-williams/.

Poems and books from Pablo Neruda: Excerpt from *Residencia en la Tierra* © Pablo Neruda 1933 & 1935 and Fundación Pablo Neruda.

Excerpts from *Residence on Earth*, copyright ©1973 by Pablo Neruda and Donald D. Walsh. Reprinted by permission of New Directions Publishing Corp.

Excerpt from *The Window Seat* reprinted by permission of HarperCollins Publishers Ltd. © 2021, Aminatta Forna.

The quotation from the poem "New Year's Morning 1965," from *Mother Muse*, is published with the permission of the author and Signal Editions/Véhicule Press.

Excerpt from *Ebony and Ivy* used with permission. © Craig Steven Wilder, 2013, *Ebony and Ivy: Race, Slavery, and the Troubled History of America's Universities*, Bloomsbury Press.

Excerpt from the PS Section of *The Book of Negroes* by Lawrence Hill © 2007 ISBN 9781443409094. Published by HarperCollins Publishers Ltd. All rights reserved.

Publisher: Meghan Macdonald | Acquiring editors: Alison Isaac and Kwame Scott Fraser | Editor: Alison Isaac
Cover designer: Laura Boyle | Cover image: Pawel Czerwinski

**Library and Archives Canada Cataloguing in Publication**

Title: Black cake, turtle soup, and other dilemmas / Gloria Blizzard.
Names: Blizzard, Gloria, author.
Description: Includes bibliographical references.
Identifiers: Canadiana (print) 20240284062 | Canadiana (ebook) 20240284143 | ISBN 9781459752801 (softcover) | ISBN 9781459752818 (PDF) | ISBN 9781459752825 (EPUB)
Subjects: LCSH: Blizzard, Gloria. | CSH: Authors, Canadian (English)—21st century—Biography. | LCGFT: Essays. | LCGFT: Autobiographies.
Classification: LCC PS8603.L59 B53 2024 | DDC C814/.6—dc23

We acknowledge the support of the Canada Council for the Arts and the Ontario Arts Council for our publishing program. We also acknowledge the financial support of the Government of Ontario, through the Ontario Book Publishing Tax Credit and Ontario Creates, and the Government of Canada.

Care has been taken to trace the ownership of copyright material used in this book. The author and the publisher welcome any information enabling them to rectify any references or credits in subsequent editions.

The publisher is not responsible for websites or their content unless they are owned by the publisher.

Printed and bound in Canada.

Dundurn Press
1382 Queen Street East
Toronto, Ontario, Canada M4L 1C9
dundurn.com, @dundurnpress

*for Merle Phyllis LaBorde Blizzard*

# Contents

III

# Preface

When I first started typing up these words, I mis-wrote "writing the truth" as "*writhing* the truth." The latter more accurately describes the complicated process of discerning the best ways of sharing my worlds.

This collection is also travel writing — from home to the hospital, up and down the subway line, into and out of the ephemeral, back and forth in time, or to a long-awaited reconnection to the Caribbean Sea.

In the tales that follow, dear reader, I introduce you to my vantage points. If you look from this hill, surrounded by these buildings, if you catch the sweet-pungent scent of guava in the ether, and if you tilt your head just slightly to the left, the blue sky becomes a cornucopia of sound and movement, and it is also so very far from blue.

***Fardeau*** *(le) is different from a burden. It is a tattered khaki-coloured knapsack full of ghosts and poisons. One can drop a fardeau. One can step over a strand of red light.*

# Black Cake Buddhism

The package weighed about fifteen pounds. I staggered with it from the concierge's desk to the elevator, noting the brownish liquid seeping through the brown craft paper and grey electrical tape. My mother had been sending such packages to me by mail twice a year since I'd moved out on my own. The first would arrive a few days before my birthday. The second delivery note from the post office would arrive a few days before Christmas. Since both occasions were in December, I would then have pounds of Trinidadian black cake in my possession. They were the envy of my friends who had either an acquired or inherited taste. A minority, like my child, hated the alcohol-infused, densely fruited mass. Others would bite into the blackened warmth and roll their eyes in ecstasy and communion with All Things Bright and Beautiful.

Then one year, it all stopped.

With an understanding that our time on earth is limited, and knowing that the deliveries would not continue forever, I'd asked my mother for the recipe many years earlier. She'd written it out for me on a sheet of lined paper with a blue ballpoint pen. I'd tucked the sheet into a cookbook and carried it with me through all my homes along Toronto's Bloor subway line: the artist-filled, soon-to-be-condemned Victorian on Sherbourne Street with a secret worm farm in the basement; the second-storey apartment on Bloor at Christie; a shared house on Milverton Boulevard, a tree-lined street just north of Coxwell and Danforth; Bloor and Keele, a few blocks from the slaughterhouses, whose existence was revealed by the invisible stench of death that made its way south on the early morning breeze; a giant brick five-bedroom home on Colbeck Street in Bloor West Village; and a bit farther north, on Annette Street, an apartment above a dog-grooming salon. I moved every two years or so, a habit entrenched in my system by the multiple moves endured during my military base–brat childhood.

"A son is yours until he finds himself a wife. A daughter is yours forever," my mum had once claimed when I was about fourteen years old. The words sounded like a trap. And I'd run from them and Caribbean girl-child prescribed roles ever since. I'd peek around the corner into the kitchen, where my mother slammed together brilliant meals while my father sat drinking with their guests. Her face was shut as she chopped, mixed, and stirred. She'd stop, wipe her hands on a red-and-white dishcloth, and exit the kitchen to sit with everyone, counting the minutes before heading back into the shadows to stir a pot or remove the dish from the oven. I'd quietly withdraw from my observation post, climb the stairs to my room, shut the door, and pick up my classical guitar, losing myself in the works of Mendelssohn and Bach. I later imagined my mother's resentment, love, and frustration slammed into each dripping package of cake that arrived from that same kitchen.

In the formerly enslaved culture of Trinidad, it would have been Black/Creole women and girls forced to cook and bake for the Spanish, French, and, finally, English enslavers. Creating the delicacy of black cake required the extensive labour of women and girls, part of a social hierarchy based on gender and race. No ingredient in Trinidadian black cake is indigenous to the island. After emancipation, I imagine some might have revelled in benefitting from their own labour and, at Christmastime, created the delicious treat for their own families, at whatever cost.

"Wouldn't it have been too expensive for people to make?" I once asked my mother. I knew that my grandmother had been a twenty-six-year-old widow with three small children in the 1940s whose husband, my grandfather, had died years earlier.

"Oh, everyone just made it happen," she said. "They just did it."

I felt the strings of patriarchy reach through the eons into my era and into my mother's statement, seeking to pull me into appropriate obedience and service, expectations that were not hoisted onto my brothers. I watched carefully which household chores, if any, they were asked to do and compared them with my own.

"She feel we discriminating," my dad laughed one day, as I scowled at yet another request to "make me a little bite," something he never asked of my brothers. I made simple dishes, the occasional batch of cookies; however, as far as more complicated endeavours like black cake, souse, and callaloo, I'd managed to avoid taking up the spatula, or the steel bowl, or the wooden spoon. Until now.

It is August. I am in the living room of my parents' Ottawa home. My mother holds a giant kitchen knife. Parang, traditional Trinidadian Christmas music, emanating from my father's computer is making her crazy. Her hymns are playing on separate devices. A noisy battle of wills. I turn off the hymns and turn down the parang.

"I can't do both," I tell them.

My mother has decades of practice with knives, and unlike me, has not cut off the tip of her own finger. Mind you, I didn't do that with a knife. I'd been using a pair of scissors to open a clear plastic one-litre bag of milk. I'd also managed to drop a weighted kitchen knife on my left foot, which required plastic surgery to rejoin the ends of a ligament that control the big toe. This was followed by months with my leg in a cast.

So many reasons to be afraid of the kitchen. Patriarchy, racism, slavery, sharp knives.

Sitting at a pullout table covered with a red plastic tablecloth, my mother and I chop the dried fruit into small bits on a wooden cutting board.

- 1 lb of currants
- 1 lb sultanas
- 1 lb Thompson raisins
- 1 lb prunes
- ¼ lb mixed peel
- 1 lb cherries (glazed)
- 2 bottles of rum (or any alcohol)

The boyfriend takes pictures of this historic event. He is encouraging. He likes eating food, any food, often cake, and figures this can't be a bad development on my part. We'd searched for almond sherry, my mother's alcohol of choice for her fruit cake, at every LCBO in the west suburban Ottawa borough of Nepean. It is in the database, said an employee, but we have not carried it here in years. We'd bought "just sherry."

My mother and I stuff the fruit into two glass jars, pour half a bottle of regular sherry into each one, twist the lids airtight, and place them "to soak" in the back of the cupboard above the fridge of my parents' kitchen. I learn that the soaking of the fruit would normally last for one year, beginning immediately after Christmas, just before attentions turned to preparations for Carnival. My mother assures me that this shortened four-month period of alcohol infusion, from August to the baking event in December, will be "just fine."

## The Body — Rupa

*When the body is standing, know that the body is standing.*

For years, the trip "home" had been infused with discomfort and anxiety. One time, I sat on the smoke-filled Greyhound bus. A small boy in the aisle across from me ate his way through a bag of Crunchits, a Turkish Delight, and a Twix bar. At some point during the five and a half hours of imposed intimacy of intercity buses, he began vomiting into a plastic bag held by his mother. I tried not to smell the acrid contents of his stomach. I looked out the window at the passing landscape of trees and more trees and swore that this time I would be able to do things differently.

I pulled out *The Eight Steps to Happiness*, by Geshe Kelsang Gyatso, from the Kadampa Buddhist tradition. I was reading it in French. Striving was a deeply ingrained paternal message, that as a Black person, I must, "work ten times as hard as everyone else." And so, I sought to enlighten myself, and to keep up my second official language skills at the same time. I scanned the book for something that would help on my trip back to Ottawa, a city I hated due to my suburban high school experience: I'd been a car-less teen, enduring long waits at bus stops, freezing in the winter, sweltering in the summer, as I tried to engage in what I perceived as the limp, tepid culture that the city had on offer.

I'd moved to Toronto after university, learning a life outside of my parents' scope of awareness and existence. The clippings that I mailed "home" — publications in small chapbooks; performances in cafés; invitations to play my songs in new cities, where

I performed both with and without shoes — were incomprehensible to them. My older brother had had his own run-ins with the arts; however, it was different for a boy to stretch his wings. I felt freak-like. Un-professioned. Un-coupled. Not quite the girl-child they had hoped for. Each trip back to the household of origin was fraught, as I intuited their wish for someone more familiar in temperament and ways.

When I'd shaved my hair off one fall: "Looks nice, G. When are you growing it back?" they'd said.

When I grew it into long dreads: "Looks nice, G," they'd said. "When are you cutting it off?"

My younger brother teased me good-naturedly by singing "She's Strange" by Cameo. A high school counsellor had once reported to me the results of her multiple-choice test booklet, designed to help me decide who I might be. Upon seeing that my results in both arts and science were exactly the same, she said, "Sorry, I can't help you." I'd spent most of my early adult life fluctuating between these two sides of myself, gaining along the way a degree in science and a diploma in fashion design, unaware of how it might be okay to be both or more.

But perhaps in Cameo's view, there was something redeeming in my way of being. The other half of the lyric was, "But I like it!" My parents rarely actively discouraged me. They just seemed resigned to waiting for these artistic impulses to go away.

With each return to the parental household, I hoped that, this time, I could be present and adult-like and not be pulled back into resentful, silent roles that usually kicked in as the bus rolled past the turn-off to Smiths Falls. I had found a short meditation on compassion in *The Eight Steps to Happiness* — breathe in all the negativity and transform it, and breathe it out again.

I imagined a return where I was confident, no longer cowed by my mother's strong beliefs, so different from my relentless spiritual and philosophical searches: Egyptology, Gurdjieff, bell hooks, shamanism, Daoism, Buddhism. One time, I revisited a church, wondering if after all these years, my mother must have been onto something. Her religion seemed to provide her with some kind of sustenance through racism, patriarchy, sexism, overwhelm, life's blows and highs. The Sunday of my visit to St. Joan of Arc on Bloor Street West, the priest called all the children present to the front of the church. As he sprinkled holy water on the awed and wiggling gaggle before him, he asked, "Do you know what this means?"

"No!" responded the chorus of voices.

"It means that you belong to Jesus Christ."

That made no sense. I left.

I continued on with my meditations, readings, spells, incense, and oils. One year, I added to my own strangeness and what felt like exile from my family of origin. After an initial foray into vegetarianism at age five, and now in light of my limited understandings of Buddhist teachings, I once again stopped eating meat.

The year of the vomit-ridden bus ride, I made it back to the parental home emotionally prepared, I thought. The table was laid with the traditional Christmas day brunch: buljol — salt fish boiled to remove some of the salt, sprinkled with oil, and garnished with tomatoes, onions, and sliced eggs. My brothers and parents were excited about digging into the delicacy.

*Slave food*, I thought petulantly, recalling the link between Newfoundland and the Caribbean — cheap salted cod to feed enslaved people, traded for cheap rum from the islands that became a Newfoundland pride called Screech. In every culture, the innovations of the lowliest, poorest, and hungriest become a cultural specialty dish: buljol in Trinidad, fish 'n' brewis in Goose Bay, Labrador, where we'd lived for one year during my early teens.

I took a piece of bake — the only part of the meal not covered in fish-soaked oil and hence the only part that I could eat — and layered it with butter. A tear leaked from the corner of my left eye. Head down, I left the table. I trudged upstairs to my childhood bedroom. I shut the door. I sat cross-legged on the floor, next to my Buddhist books, and tried out my new meditation practice. It did not help.

## El Dorado

*Gold. A mineral. A body. An emotional weight.*

The fruit has soaked for four months; I've returned to finish the cake. I can't find a grater, a measuring spoon, a bowl for the nuts. "Shit," I say. Someone else's kitchen always involves relentlessly opening and closing cupboard doors. My mother points to the second cupboard from the left, top shelf, where I find a giant silver bowl.

"We didn't have metal bowls in my time. They were enamel. Red earthenware maybe," she says.

I take it down. I've made some sorrel and am diluting the tart red liquid with water and sugar for us to enjoy as we undertake this final stage of baking the black cake. Sorrel is another tradition that I've picked up this year. I give her a teaspoon periodically to taste.

"More sugar," she says. "Just a bit more. Some more."

My father takes two heaping teaspoons with each cup of tea. He is diabetic. He is ninety-two years old. He sits in front of the computer, his only view out into the world, except for the occasional medical appointment — an ordeal involving special taxis booked weeks in advance by his eighty-eight-year-old wife. He used to dominate every room he entered. Now, he is fading in plain sight. He sips what seem like pounds of the white gold that had led circuitously to the existence of my mixed-race Caribbean family and to his current physical state.

My mother places yet another cup before my father in response to his occasional spirited demand for more "Tea!"

"The golden age is not golden," she will tell me when out of his auditory range. "I'm so tired. I'm ready for this to stop."

## Vedanā

*An awareness of mental, emotional, and physical states.*

At a very young age, I became aware of my mother's suffering. She was doing too much, running a medical office and managing a household with three children. Like all kids, I tracked her moods; my survival depended on it. She drove, she organized, she cooked. At least she did not also wash. Gwendolyn the washer woman did the weekly washing in a concrete sink out back and hung it on a line between the shaddock and the orange trees.

Like monk and writer Thomas Merton, she'd become Catholic by choice. She and her siblings lived with their grandmother after the death of both parents. Every Sunday, a neighbouring family, the Dominics, would invite her to join them on the walk down the hill to Eastern Main Road to attend mass at St. Elizabeth Church. Something about the ceremony and teachings struck her profoundly, and she took the training to formally join the church at the age of fifteen.

She had provided me with perfectly good culture, traditions, and religion. Perhaps she experienced my drifting away as a deep affront, and the meals where I was not fully welcome were an expression of this. After all, I had been named for the church. After vetoing the names Noelle and Carol, my mother heard "Gloria in excelsis Deo" on the radio as she lay in her birthing bed. "That's it! Gloria!" she remembers exclaiming. I am also the namesake of a motherly nun who took care of her during her hospital stay. My middle name is Anne, with an *e*.

## The Mind-Citta

*See that the mind went out to think.*

My trip home to complete the cake is my first return for Christmas holidays in years. This time, I do not cling to my books and meditation techniques, my oils and incense. This time, I feel brave and secure with my boyfriend at the wheel of a crumbling grey Honda CR-V. I do not sink into insecurities as we roll past Smiths Falls.

My father is in a world parallel to the cake preparations. He sits in his wheelchair in front of his computer, looking at YouTube videos from Trinidad. Parang fills the room. He calls us over to look at a group from the Carib (Kalinago) village of Lopinot, playing cuatros, shak shaks, singing about the Virgin Mary in Spanish. My mother moves from her armchair to a straight-backed chair and places herself at the head of the folding table covered with bowls, spoons, a bag of flour, sugar, butter, a cardboard container of twelve eggs, a handful of almonds, a tin of baking soda, and a small bottle of pure vanilla essence. I pull the two jars of sherry-infused fruit from the back of the cupboard over the fridge.

I tell her that I am nervous about the burning of the sugar and setting off smoke alarms.

"Oh, you don't have to burn sugar anymore. You just use browning." She hands me a small jar that her friend Cynthia left for me.

I am both relieved and disappointed. I wanted the drama of thick, grey smoke permeating the home and the acrid smell that hinted at the slightly bitter taste that lingered in the cakes of my childhood. *Browning* sounds suspicious, like an MSG-laced food-like substance far away from my childhood sensory memories.

"Cream the butter until you can't hear the sugar anymore," she says. Her role is only to direct, yet she can't stop herself from reaching for a spoon to help stir.

"How much browning?" I ask my mother as I mix the flour into the creamed sugar and butter.

"Until it's brown," she says.

I sigh. She sighs. She is upset with my father. She is tired of caring for him and yet cannot accept the help that I try to provide. I tell her of a Buddhist belief, that at the moment of death, one must be in a good mood, as this state of mind determines where you go next. She smiles. She orders the greasing of the two round pans with Crisco and the lining of them with parchment paper. I pour the batter, filling each pan to just over halfway.

"The cake is baking. You said a long, slow cook. How long?"

"Until the cake pulls away from the sides of the pan," she says.

"How long is that?"

"No idea."

The parang surrounding us is getting louder. Hymns emanate from the CD player next to the couch. This time, I go to my father, at his station, and turn off the parang. I leave my mother's hymns on low.

## Dhamma

*How things actually are.*

My mother was twelve years old when her mother died suddenly. My mother had two younger siblings. She found the pieces of skirts, pinafores, pants, and shorts for new school uniforms that their mother had cut and laid aside. She pinned the pieces together and ran them under the presser foot of the black Singer sewing machine, her thin brown feet powering it by pushing the foot pedal back and forth. She taught me to sew when I was twelve.

She did not, however, teach me (or my brothers) how to cook. She threw brilliant meals together, working too fast to involve us in her preparations. She made curries and pelau and what I perceived as the miracle meal, feeding a family of five with one five-ounce can of tuna. She'd cut it with stewed tomatoes, greens, and spices to make a sauce that was placed over a bed of white rice. When years later I saw a university roommate eat a full can of tuna herself, I was astounded. I did not know that was possible or even desirable. I suspect that my mother had had the benefit of her grandmother's coaching and had not figured this cooking business out all on her own. It took me years of sorting through cookbooks to figure out the basics. I also chose men who cooked exceedingly well, and I studied their ease in the kitchen with awe. I had an odd ability to create imaginative and delicious meals that occurred only over an open fire while camping in old-growth Ontario forests.

"You know you can't live on just cake, right?" I told my twelve-year-old child one day. They only liked baking. I looked at the cake recipe book, covered in hardened splatters of yellow batter. We'd tried out pies, white cakes, yellow cakes, chocolate and vanilla icings. My mother had not had such hours to bake and cook with a child. She was under different pressures. She did not have the freedom of time to spend guiding small hands to measure, pour, and stir.

"You have to know how to feed yourself. I need to ensure that you can make at least two meals. Let's do this together. Cut," I remember saying as I handed them a knife, a block of tofu, some garlic. We made a stir fry. They scowled through it all. Resentment is a good emotion. Resentment leads to dinner.

Sometimes I crave the foods of my childhood. I chop up an onion, crush some garlic, add thyme, cumin, curry, coconut milk, and then open a can of red beans instead of pigeon peas. I slice a plump, rich yellow zaboca, add a knife-full of kuchela to the side of the plate. Sometimes, I fry up some bake. Wheat, flour, and oil. Bake, like bannock, fills bellies with fried starches.

## The Eucharist

*The body and blood of Christ. Usually ingested on a Sunday morning.*

The Christmas package arrives by mail to my most recent home, in Parkdale, where the neighbourhood public library housed the rise of Toronto's Black and Caribbean literati in the 1960s and '70s.

"Monk's cake. It's good! You buy it from the Cistercian monks," my mother says. She has replaced the heavy packages of homemade black cake with small parcels containing tiny fruit-laden loaves made by men of her religious tradition — as far as I know, no female labour is involved.

"Poor rum over it and let it soak for a few days," she advises.

I now know that it is possible to make a vegetarian version of many traditional Trinidadian dishes, and I make buljol using canned jackfruit instead of dried salted cod. My child is grown and has their own household, where they bake expertly and cook almost exclusively tortellini and baked root vegetables.

In response to my wandering life, a difficult marriage, and other dramas, several empathetic healers have asked me, "How did you manage?" Or more bluntly, "Why are you not crazy?" Reiki. Meditation. Dance. Music. Buddhism. I pick an answer, depending on who is asking. The truth might be that I was sustained by cake. Through all the distance and misunderstanding, my mother mailed pounds of black cake twice a year until I didn't need to receive it anymore and she no longer needed to send it. Maybe the process of feeding each other kindness, compassion, love, tenderness, dinner, and cake is both a Buddhist temple and a Catholic church.

My mother also mailed annual Advent cards. "Why does Grandma keep sending these when we are not Christian?" my child asked one year as they opened up the first of twenty-four cardboard windows, one to be opened each day in the countdown to the day of Christ's birth. They pulled out the sugary chocolate treat and popped it into their mouth.

"I don't know," I remember saying. "Good chocolate?"

"Mm hmm," they nodded and chewed.

# Ghost

Even at nine years old I questioned the wisdom of parading that Trinidad Carnival. I thought we were trying to stay safe, and I was hardly low-key wearing a giant costume covered in gold sequins and beads. Long tufts of coki-yea, the woody midsection from the leaves of a coconut tree, extended my girth to about six feet in every direction. Dad said he'd done nothing wrong; he had the right to participate in the culture, he wasn't hiding. He'd commissioned ornate individual costumes for my little brother and I and then, as he'd said, "taken the necessary precautions." In my case this meant providing me with a bodyguard named Stuart. My father introduced us to each other and then disappeared into the crowds, shirtless with a flask of rum strung around his neck to jump up and play mas'. I looked up into the hundreds of faces of costumed and bejewelled revellers around me. I looked at Stuart.

He was tall and large with very dark skin. His job was to be with me the entire length of the parade. This worked well, except when I needed to cross the stage for the competition. That I did alone, pulling my heavily costumed self up the wooden ramp to wait for my name, costume, and band to be called. I then launched myself toward centre stage of the Red Cross Kiddies Carnival, chipping in time to the calypso road march, shaking the costume in front of the judges. I spun around, dancing back and forth across the full width of the stage, flashing gold in the sunlight and shaking my coki-yea fronds for the audience. Playing a big mas' was an important rite of passage, my father had told us. "You have to know who you are and where you come from." Maybe he already knew that this would be our last Carnival on the island.

By the time we did pack out, I knew why we were leaving. Three thousand night raids had been executed on family homes of the politically disobedient. To date, we had avoided an invasion and a ransacking; however, by this time, incidents had been adding up. The light aeroplane my dad flew on weekends was a red-and-white Cessna 150. One day, its engine stalled mid-flight, as the air uptake valve had mysteriously been covered with a cap. The result was that the plane's gas tank collapsed in on itself. The plane started to fall out of the sky. My father crash-landed the small two-seater on a dirt road just outside the village of Moruga, placing the plane's wheels six inches from the weed-filled ditches on either side. "Air force training," he said. "Do it right the first time."

Another day, he showed us numbers on a lab report confirming near-fatal levels of arsenic in his hair and fingernails. With his medical training, he'd determined that the white powder, a common weapon used in southern climes, must have been consistently added to his system on a regular basis. He had one person in mind who was often at their office.

After tampered brakes in our white Volkswagen buggy left my parents careening down a curving hill, slowing, coming to a stop only due to a flat section of road and an interaction with some bushes, they knew it was time to go.

Dad left first. My mother refused to leave right away. "It's not me they are after," she said. She insisted that we finish the academic year in our various schools. The prospect of showing up in Canada in mid-June with three disoriented kids made her brave enough to stay put for a couple extra weeks. She sold everything she could from the medical office and our home.

Then there was Dawn, our simple-minded Alsatian with a sway back, a mild disposition, and a paucity of mothering skills. Most of her litter had died as she would rise suddenly and stumble over the nursing puppies who fell from her teats. We needed someone to take her. Gabriel, a distant cousin, needed a guard dog or at least the appearance of one. We dropped Dawn off with him the day before our departure. As we drove away, I turned for a last look at our furry simpleton. She stood tall, tail erect for the first time, watching us through the wrought iron gate.

On our final day, my mother handed us each a small suitcase to take to a waiting car. As I'd had a thoroughly colonial upbringing that included embroidery, netball, and English folk songs, I could not bring myself to fits and howls of protest. Instead, at some point during the drive to Piarco International Airport, on our way to Goose Bay, Labrador, Canada, I simply stopped speaking.

•

At some point during the previous year, my younger brother and I had been engaged in a favourite and covert activity — jumping on our parents' bed. In the midst of our glee, a hard, shiny black object slid from beneath our father's pillow, down the length of the polycotton sheet to nestle between us. We halted our exuberance and looked at each other. I picked up the gun. I put it back down.

This was the evidence that my then skeptical child-self needed. Maybe, we really were in some kind of trouble. The rantings about subterfuge were connected to the world outside of us and were not just in my father's head. In the solipsistic stance of childhood, I'd figured he was just being weird and trying to make us all tense and unhappy. Now, I saw that the gun might be needed to point toward something. Maybe the revealed threat and whispered parental panic had a source. However, even with the weight of the gun in my small hands, I fought cognitively against this new understanding. *This is stupid*, I thought.

We called out to our mother. She came running. We protested its presence. Why? we demanded. Why is there a gun under Dad's pillow? Mostly I protested that it was so close to her head, imagining that if it went off, it might leave us motherless.

Our mother shrugged, a helpless tilt of her head.

•

In 2009, Selwyn D. Ryan published a book called *Eric Williams: The Myth and the Man*, with the University of the West Indies Press. My father had handed it to me as I sat on the beige sofa bed, where I often perched on visits to my parents' Ottawa home. As I skimmed through the 842-page tome, I came across a paragraph:

> Between 1972 and 1974 there were numerous manhunts, as well as searches of homes, some belonging to prominent people including two doctors and a permanent secretary. The searches, which were often executed by the dreaded "Flying Squad" under the leadership of the assistant commissioner, Randolph Burroughs, were carried on amid great show of force, and invariably nothing was found to justify the brutality.[1]

My father underlined and wrote in every book that he read. Written above the year 1974, he'd penciled in "1975." "There has been much controversy as to how much of this Williams knew and condoned," the book states. Burroughs, appointed by Williams to the position, was a name I heard often around our fraught family dinners as my father had expounded on his experiences of that time. For the first time, with book in hand, I felt that my childhood memories of the era had been externally organized. My father had not just been difficult or paranoid or crazy. The stories floating through the air around us kids, the unclear rationale for the breach in my early life, the phantasmic tales of subterfuge doubted by many had been named. I looked up at him and asked, "Does this paragraph refer to us?"

"No," he said. "We were never raided. One soldier told his commanding officer, 'I'm not raiding doc's house.' The plan was abandoned." A raid did not happen that night — to us.

•

In 1962, the newly minted independent nation of Trinidad and Tobago had a new leader. Eric Williams was brilliant. He'd attended the most prestigious academies of Empire, was Oxford educated, had garnered a Ph.D. He had deep understanding of these worlds and had written on the intricate connections between capitalism and slavery. He understood this new nation was founded on the lands and lives of the Taino, the Kalinago (Caribs), and other nations; the theft of the lives of enslaved peoples from Africa; indentured labourers from India and China; and smatterings of others. The small Caribbean nation of Trinidad and Tobago was now led by a Black man with vision and plans. The United States, by contrast, was a seething wreck of denial and obfuscation about its roots. It was hosing down and setting dogs on Black people who objected to living at the bottom of their caste system.

My parents, who'd settled in Canada, and other Trinidadians ensconced around the world, were quickly drawn into the excitement of new nationhood. The national anthem began, "Forged from the love of liberty, in the fires of hope and prayer ... Let every creed and race find an equal place." And so on. Those must have been heady times.

"The plan was always to go home," my mother says. By 1966, my father had accepted a job with the Trinidad and Tobago Regiment, caring for soldiers. My mother returned to the island ahead of him with us three children. She wanted to get back by a certain time, so that my older brother could sit his common entrance exam, a nationwide test for eleven-year-olds that could determine your future. In preparation, each morning before school, my father had woken him up and trained him in mathematics. He knew that what my brother had learned so far in the Canadian system would be no match for the rigorous British model of education on the island. And as the son of Steve Blizzard, who'd competed for and won an island scholarship to study abroad, my brother had to pass for a good school. We arrived, he killed it — the exam, I mean. My brother. He pulled it off. He was brilliant then. Still is.

My mother also executed another of their ideas. My father would later claim that he left Canada one day and opened up an office in Belmont the next morning. What he always neglected to mention was that his wife had been in Trinidad for months, working at Community Hospital, finding and setting up a home for their three children, putting us into schools, arranging transportation to and from, and managing the household. She also commuted daily to the nascent medical office on Erthig Road, to ensure that it was constructed properly.

The job with the Regiment never materialized. My father was disappointed and outraged. And without the promised job that had initiated our return to the island, the medical office became the one source of family income. The family struggled financially, partly because my parents treated everyone who came into the office, even those who could not pay. My mother recalls ducking out to the pharmacy around the corner, to buy medication for patients she knew would never be able to buy it themselves. Several times, patients showed up injured at their office. It might have been the head wound that bled like a demon or the ectopic pregnancy that my mother, a trained midwife, spotted in an instant. If they could not treat them on site, my parents packed them into their white Volkswagen buggy and drove them to the hospital. Invariably, upon return, the remaining patients had cleaned up the blood from the office floor and were sitting there calmly waiting for their turn to be seen.

By the late '60s and early '70s, my parents had garnered some goodwill and influence. However, they'd also attracted some bad mindedness. At five foot six, my father seemed much larger than this. And with a tinkling rum and Coke and the requisite off-white shirt-jac, he could hold the attention of a room. He'd tell jokes or sing an ole-time calypso. Contrastingly, he also railed loudly against those who had upset him. Was it true he was asked to join the political game? Was it true that he'd refused contemptuously with, "No. Y'all too corrupt"?

"He brought it on himself," I heard years later. "He kept talking. Loudly."

•

A haunting can be a repeated story. Each time you run a tale in your head, the body experiences it in real time and creates the hormones of flight. Neurons form dedicated pathways and even seek to relive familiar discomforts. By 1976, we were back in Canada, the land of my birth. And over the next ten years, my father debriefed at home, his trauma landing in the ears and bodies of his interlocutors, the children still at home, and his wife who'd quietly slept with a gun pointed at her head.

"They t'ief!" my dad would exclaim, answering his own query at the dinner table. We all sat and watched him. He'd set up his own answer with the following questions: "How so-and-so could say, 'I could buy Trinidad'?" "How so-and-so could own skyscrapers in Canada?" We occasionally egged him on with a familiar question. His voice would get louder at this opportunity to explain to us, again, what we well knew.

A haunting can be a feeling of no real recourse, a memory of strange goings-on, a suspicion that the ground upon which we stand is warped. Who can one trust? What is real? Who would believe you if it were? I grew up with this in my mind at all times. I became haunted, carrying a generalized fear around in my bones. Regardless of fact, fiction, history, imagination, or story, in my child-mind, it was because of Eric Williams that our lives had been disrupted. I was resentful of that name. For years, I remained mad at my father as well, as I resented the need to return to Canada. I'd arrived on the island with my Canadian accent, not quite Trini enough. Upon return to Canada, I slid halfway back into the accent with which I'd first learned to speak. I hated leaving my familiar being on the island, to once again become foreign. I learned to live in a generalized non-belonging, a kind of imagined invisibility. It took me decades to land.

I felt a familiar jolt in my system when I read in the *Guardian* that the seminal work of Dr. Eric Williams, *Capitalism and Slavery*, was to be reissued by a major press. My child-self was still discombobulated by that name. I knew that I would write to clear this breach of spirit. Old harms train us. They can keep us circling like dogs on a spot of ground or they can lead us to new terrain. We choose. They can whisper toxins from the depths of memory or they can inhabit us with wisdom.

I am still reading the tome on the contested legacy of the former prime minister of Trinidad and Tobago. I will reread the great treatise, *Capitalism and Slavery*. I will read it again even though I can just barely separate art from spectre.

# Turtle Soup

"It's not a good death," scientist Jory Mullen tells me. "The brain keeps working even when the body is in pieces. I have to bash the head in with a rock to stop the suffering from continuing for days as the head lies there in the sun, rain, or cold." She tells me that she has seen people aim the wheels of their vehicles to run over a turtle and that "three percent of drivers will swerve to hit one," a number determined by a study using decoys on an Ontario roadway. It is called "popping," she tells me. As the dorsally located lungs explode, they make a loud sound that some find amusing. Some people poach turtles to serve as a specialty in restaurants. Others engage in "plinking," shooting at their shells for the fun of making another pleasant sound. Sometimes the bullets pierce the shell, reaching the internal organs.

As a kid, I'd witnessed death — that of a chicken killed in our backyard. We lived on Senior Street, Trinidad, on the first floor of a two-storey off-white concrete structure. It had an inexplicably flat-roofed design found only in the tropics that ensured that in-habitants were constantly heated. My brothers and I had once watched as a neighbour held a chicken still with one hand and expertly cut off its head with a cutlass in the other. The body ran around, headless, synapses firing; however, the brain was dead, eyes unseeing and dulled. Turtles are different. The eyes of a decapitated head keep rolling and looking, synapses feeling, searching for an end to relentless, bodiless pain.

We shared a backyard of scrub grass and small stones with Mama and Papa Ho and their five children. One day I noted that they'd placed a small dark brown wooden box on the outer wall of our downstairs flat. A long-nailed scaly foot poked out from between the slats. One of the Ho kids lifted the lid to reveal the dappled shell and curious, reaching neck of a Julie mango–sized turtle, scrambling against the walls of its confinement. The middle boy proudly showed my brothers and I how to feed it crunchy scraps of green vegetables. I don't know what their parents did for a living. I did know that this was a struggling neighbourhood. We were poor–not poor, in the inexplicable way that some of us educated colonial subjects can be. Certificated and degreed up the yingyang but missing the details on the building of capital or wealth — a different education that was not on offer. In our case, we lived in rented houses in odd neighbourhoods. Our mother pressed against the wooden slats of inexplicable struggle. Her husband was a doctor after all, and she, a nurse midwife. And yet she scrambled to get the kids uniformed and schooled. The right elementary school could determine your future. The right high school would certainly do so. Education, we were told, was always the way forward. Meanwhile, in our scrappy yard, my little brother and I had other more important things in mind, such as playing with the cat's newborn kittens even though we'd been told not to touch them. The mother cat soon rejected them and ate their bodies, leaving little heads for us to find when we returned to play with them one morning.

One day, Papa Ho came down to share a special treat with us. "Turtle soup," he said proudly, holding out a spoon of brownish stew for us to taste. My five-year-old self slowly made a horrified connection to the animal in the wooden box out back. I refused the soup and ran outside to check. It was empty of course.

From that point on, I wanted nothing to do with cooked flesh, pets or otherwise. No chicken, no beef, no fish, no turtle. My parents were resigned. My brothers watched side-eye as I ate rice and gravy at dinner. This quickly expanded to no gravy as I realized that it was essentially what I called "meat juice." Meals were tortuous. I ate plates of white rice as wafts of my mother's stewed chicken filled the house. I remained resolute in my protest, a characteristic that my family assures me I had from birth.

•

The appearance of this new meal made overt an underlying unsafety in the world. If pets could become dinner, then what else could happen? I had already sensed that all was not well, that things were not as they seemed.

Down the street, on La Puerta Avenue, lived my mother's best friend, Aunty June. Scottish in origin, she and her four children had been deposited on the island by her Trinidadian husband while he completed post-graduate dental studies in Edinburgh. My mother managed her own three kids while my father completed medical work in Canada. These two professional women — nurses with several children each — managed jobs, households, and children, their labour supporting the careers of professional men.

Aunty June, my mother, Merle, and a third close friend, Aunty Lynn, worked as a coven. Aunty Lynn drove us to Bishop Anstey

Private School and looked after my one-year-old brother, Carlos, while my mother and Aunty June worked at Community Hospital. Not much was explained to us children. We were protected through not-telling; however, something of a deeper world always snuck through as we tracked the glances, avoidances, moods, and energy levels of our exhausted mothers. Perhaps my five-year-old brain imagined that on some level I could help — no meat, less slaughter, less inexplicable pain.

•

I was awfully hungry after a week or two of rice. My mother, unsure of what to do with this newly vegetarian child, had continued cooking for the family as usual — Trinidadian dishes of pelau and stewed chicken and curried beef, bake, and buljol. Perhaps feeling sorry for me, she offered some butter to add to my rice, for a bit of flavour. I grew hungry and soon gave up my new lifestyle, returning to dinners as usual at the family table. My brothers watched suspiciously to see "what will she do now." I ate the delicious-smelling stewed chicken and curried beef.

One night, after my father returned from Canada, he and my mother raced toward Community Hospital in a white Volkswagen buggy with a woman in agony in the back seat — an ectopic pregnancy. She died in the car. One day, Aunty June's son Larry cut his foot on a bit of glass in our scrappy yard. My father unceremoniously opened up his black leather doctor's bag, injected a local anesthetic, then pulled out his needle and thread and sewed up the wound as my little brother, the Ho children, and I watched with interest.

We do what we can when circumstances reveal themselves.

I didn't become vegetarian again until many years later. No chicken. No cow. No pig. No turtle. I'd gathered bits of information on the impacts of large-scale farming techniques on climate change. I'd seen images of the inside of a slaughterhouse and videos of terrified animals following the stench of terror to their imminent deaths. I'd meandered into some Buddhist studies on compassion. Slowly, over years, I eliminated beef, then chicken, then fish from my diet. Pork was last to go. I enjoyed frying it slowly with soy sauce, the soft texture of the slightly overcooked flesh as it fell apart in my mouth.

•

Between May and October every summer, Jory is on call. She gathers up turtles that have been injured or killed on Ontario roads. Popped. Plinked. Poached. Run over. If a turtle can be saved, she takes it home and gives it fluids until it can be transported to the Turtle Hospital in Peterborough. Sometimes the creature is dead. Then, if female, Jory will harvest the eggs from the body, incubate them, and raise them until they are old enough to re-enter the Ontario wetlands and forests. If the body on the road has been in the sun for too long, however, the eggs inside are essentially cooked. Jory is vegan. No chicken. No cow. No pig. No turtle. No eggs. She shows me a picture she's taken, of a baby turtle clambering out of its shell. "See, it has a tooth on its face that it uses to break and hack itself out of its shell. Then the tooth falls off. Cute," she says.

# The Yellow Dress

*Oxum, the Afro-Brazilian goddess of fresh water, embodies the beauty of a trickling stream and the grandness of a waterfall. She carries a mirror to adore herself in one hand. In the other she carries her warrior-dagger. She wears a long yellow dress.*

I stood still for the fitting, pins scratching softly at my skin with each intake of breath. We, my mother and I, were in the seamstress's living room. I held my upper arms aloft as if preparing for flight, as she cut the arm holes into the shift of soft, pale yellow fabric. There was something spell-like in her craft as she spun me slowly, expertly removing slivers from the arm holes with her giant scissors, no patterns required. The fabric, with its silky sheen, felt cool and smooth against my skin. A magical, covert process — that I might call the evolution of girl-ness — was also taking place as we waited for the dress to take form. We picked up the fully formed dress two weeks later.

The day I was to wear it was approaching rapidly. I recall that my hair behaved particularly well the day of the ceremony. It was confirmation time at the church on Gloster Lodge Road. However, when the time came to put on my yellow dress, something did not feel right. Perhaps I sensed the psychic weight of the ritual's requirement for prettiness, a required silky girl-ness, the process of preparation as if for a wedding or a feast, with me, the meal to be consumed. That day, I put my new dress on grudgingly and joined the ceremony, the anointing of foreheads with oil. My mother had carefully parted my hair, greased it, weaving French braids on either side of my head. This was the most mature hairdo that I'd had to date, in contrast to the two plaits with bright red ribbons on each end that I usually wore to school. I held my head high. I would not let my photograph be taken, however, and turned away quickly from the snap of any camera. I was proud and yet embarrassed at the primping and preparation for presentation at the altar.

At that age — I was eleven — girls start to note the deal that's been attached to their very being without their participation or consent. I recall a craving to be barebacked in the rain like my little brother, the warm droplets slamming onto my chest, with a touch of cool wind, but could not bring myself to shed my blouse, despite my mother's words to "go ahead — if you really want to," an addendum whose subtext I heard as a caution, not permission. Message received.

The crawl space under the house on Hermitage Road was not really a space for girls either; however, I spent hours there with my little brother, or on the galvanized iron garage roof, where we could pluck the half ripe guavas hanging within easy reach of our fingers. We'd fill ourselves with the pink seed-filled flesh and the pithy tart exterior that made our faces pucker. A year later, I clambered down from the garage roof for another special event. My mother had arranged for a birthday tea party for me at Trinidad's Hilton Hotel.

My friends and I wore our best dresses. We had ornamented cakes and vanilla ice cream. Unfortunately, the hotel's air conditioning was at its highest setting — mostly what I remember was being very, very cold in a pretty, sleeveless dress. Pretty clothing does not always serve the self, I learned. I cupped my hands around my hot tea and thought of the hot sun outside. I might have been dreaming of a more regular pursuit, like sitting in the branches of a guava tree, or crouching in the yard over Dawn, the family dog, my little brother and I pulling the ticks off her skin and squishing them into the ground, creating bloody spots of earth.

A few years before confirmation, my mother had used her sewing skills to make the wardrobe for another church ceremony. She'd carefully cut the white train of her wedding dress and crafted the tiny garment on the black Singer sewing machine. For all three of her children, she dressed us in this same silken gown that flowed past our tiny feet. At three weeks of age, we were each held in our mother's arms for this ritual welcome into Catholicism. She would remove the silken cap from our heads so that the priest could pour water on our newborn selves. The intention was to cleanse us of the stain of original sin.

"I changed the colour of the ribbon in the cap for each baby," she added proudly. Blue for the first child. Pink for me. Blue ribbons for my little brother who followed.

Later, at the prestigious Bishop Anstey High School, I presented in the uniform — a blue skirt, white shirt, and a red-and-black tie. We also wore a strange felt hat, somewhere between a nurse's cap and the tricorne of a British colonial uniform made of blue felt. The impossible crown of felt sat perched on the tops of our heads. They were not beloved and were often accidentally-on-purpose misplaced by the all-girl school population. At that time, along with regular academics of mathematics, science, composition, and such, we were taught the skills of ladies of Empire like hand sewing small objects and the art of embroidery. I chose my decorative stitches carefully. I loved to run the thick colourful threads through squares of cotton, making lines of running, feather, knot, satin, backstitch, and sewing a blanket stitch around the edges.

The first useful piece that I sewed myself was a teal-coloured handbag that I decorated with dark purple and lilac stitching. I slung its white rope handle proudly over one shoulder at important preteen gatherings. My pièce de résistance, however, was a yellow pillowcase upon which I'd drawn a rose in the top right corner and embroidered it with a pink running stitch. It was important, the choosing of fabric. Bending over choices of texture, colour, and stiches with which to adorn it — these were artful choices. I created small, intricate worlds, exhibiting an agency that I did not feel when I looked up.

"It's time to learn to sew on the machine," said my mother. I may have been pulled indoors from one of my other tasks — standing on a fence and flying a chickichong made of tissue paper and coki-yea, a fragile type of kite. I'd been pestering her to show me how to sew for some time. And the time was now. She turned on the minute bulb of the black Singer sewing machine. She wound the thread through a complicated network of steel loops and holes, into the needle that would pierce the fabric repeatedly, forming uniform backstitch in a perfectly straight line. I loved the process of choosing a pattern, laying the delicate paper on fabric folded on the grain or bias, and then pinning the layers of fabric and paper together with straight pins. It seemed very important to hold a plethora of pins between your lips, points in, heads out, for rapid access and efficient pinning. It seemed, this process, a rite of passage into womanly adornment. I was twelve. I liked this part of girl-training and negotiated my way in and out of various templates of adornment, creating dresses, jumpers (culottes, we called them), skirts, and blouses.

My mother's important dresses, by contrast, were always floor-length maxis, sewn by the same maker of my yellow dress. I'm sure many times, she stood, upper arms held aloft like wings, for her fittings. The dresses were made of polyester blends mostly, and the popular new invention, crimplene. It was a bit thicker and held all body parts into smoothness. Did she feel she could fly? My brother and I would watch in awe as she got ready to go out at night with our father. The long, flowing dresses, the earrings, the lipstick.

My own sewing and embroidered creations held a gesture toward adventure that I'd witnessed in books. Enid Blyton's Famous Five series featured five kids solving mysteries somewhere in the English countryside. They held the attention of me and my group of friends. We traded and gifted these books to each other for birthdays. Duncan McLaren, in his memoir *Looking for Enid*, writes on his obsession with Blyton, and reveals that like me, many others identified with and were taken by the character Georgina. Georgina, George for short, wore pants and had a close-cropped haircut, and was knowledgeable and adventurous. The other girl in the group, Anne, wore dresses, and was a small, soft young girl who could only follow along behind the others. Anne did not have great ideas on solving the mysteries. By contrast, what the character George conveyed to me was that in order to be adventurous, one must have the appropriate attire.

The fact that the two were white girls was not significant to me or any of my friends. I was not yet in a space where I questioned representation. And outside my home, in our real world, people like us were in all strata of Caribbean society. To us, it was a good story, and either way, that's what was on offer. I could see, however, in the illustrations throughout the book, that adventure and speaking out were accompanied by short hair and pants. In that world, a yellow dress for which you stood pinned into stillness, might mean something else entirely.

"Her gift to the world is a shared cultural heritage,"[1] says the writer McLaren in his study on Blyton. And on our commonwealth island, steeped in British tradition, we joined in. Just like little boys and girls in England, we carefully wrapped our new school textbooks in brown paper for preservation, respecting the word. We dutifully protected and prepared the books for reuse and transmission of the ideas held within them. We were unwittingly of the shared cultural heritage where Ragamuffin Jo, the only girl character who might have resembled us physically in hue, was called names, taken for a boy, excluded from the group of white children, and punched in the face.

La Diablesse or Ladjablès is a Trinidadian folkloric character, a woman who has one normal foot and one cloven hoof, a Black woman. In the video series Trinbago Stories,[2] author and historian Gérard Besson suggests that the entity is a European distortion of Erzulie, the Goddess of Love. It reveals much fear of womanhood and of Blackness, both of which were seen as being fundamentally evil. I remember as a very young woman feeling that perhaps this might be true, that I was exactly that — fundamentally evil. Cultural transmission received.

In Richardo Keens-Douglas's children's book *La Diablesse and the Baby*, she is illustrated as a beautiful woman with smooth dark skin, an insistent and powerful force in a wide-brimmed hat tilted coquettishly over one eye. In this version of the story, La Diablesse repeatedly asks the grandmother to give over her grandchild, as she just wants to hold the baby. The grandmother, however, senses that the insistent ask is an attempt to steal the child. She trusts her intuition and sends La Diablesse away.

In other manifestations, La Diablesse wears a long white maxi dress, her head wrapped in a crowning swath of white fabric. Her clothing contrasts with the night sky as she walks at the edge of the roadway, her human foot on the asphalt, her hooved foot on the earth at the side so that the hoof's clop cannot be heard. La Diablesse expresses another kind of agency. A wayward man accompanies her down a dark road. She enacts a social correction, a revenge of the harmed. When the man stops to light his cigarette, upon striking the match, he disappears in a puff of smoke. I somehow held these stories in my system, protected through vicious times and psychic blows, with the possibility that any man who would harm a woman or a child would disappear. La Diablesse is righteous rage and action for those who can only escape in their dreams.

The Famous Five series oddly shaped my worlds almost as much as the tales of La Diablesse, the blood-sucking Soucouyant, the Moko Jumbies, and the Douens with their backward-facing feet. While my preteen self saw the fictional character George lead the way, deeply embedded in my ancestral memory is also the power of these supernatural creatures. Both books and tales filled my head with possibilities. Escape from trouble or the very concrete blows of racism and patriarchy was perhaps within our ken. Even as I felt the weight of distortion of femaleness or the pressure to perform girl-ness, prettiness, obedience, and order, I also knew that I, too, could live beyond what surrounded me. I knew that we need not always be lost.

When I first entered a deep focus on poetry, music, and performance, my costumes for these artistic adventures were crafted from disparate pieces: coats from the Sally Ann; jeans from a department store; the occasional high-priced find, a second-hand designer blouse or bracelet; running shoes; earrings that dangled and shone; and always a bit of whimsy — a crochet scarf or a delicate hand-embroidered kerchief that I held close to my heart. My mother called these concoctions "calculated undress."

Women, we exist under a weight of perpetual gaze. A date once offered to buy me a whole new wardrobe, to replace my carefully calculated undress with pieces more form fitting, as there was not enough body revealed. Never quite right for someone. I now note how young women try to find themselves. They wish for joy and yet brace for what the world might throw at their very selves: expectations, opinions; judgement of body, attire, and presentation. It took a while to get here, and I'm glad that I now live further from that place. I have not, however, eliminated entirely the deep self-consciousness installed early. These patterns instilled on our psyches die hard. Mostly, I wear whatever I like. I am less a presentation of something to be consumed and mostly don't care much what someone might think of how I sit, stand, dress, think, dance, don't dance. I am also more likely to wear a long gown. A maxi. I do not yet have a yellow one. That's coming. Maybe I'll find a special seamstress who will make one for me, or I'll pull out my sewing machine and make it myself. Protection can be crafted even as there are still openings where the harm or the light or the ancestors get through.

I am alternately wrapped in cozy comfort or casting off garments that no longer serve me. I am part goddess, part tea drinker. Our mothers live within us — even as we must outrun them. I have two of my mother's maxi dresses. They are beautiful. They fit me well. One is of firm body-shaping crimplene. The other is of softest flowing polyester that looks like silk.

# Hummingbird

I learned early the power of silence. At three years old, I could send my father into conniptions by not saying "good morning." I'd peek out at him from behind my mother's legs as my older brother begged, in his mind, for me to just say good morning, so he could eat his breakfast in peace. (I'd observed how the world worked "from small.") To excuse such unwieldly behaviours, this girl-child was given the label "shy."

Over time, I noted where else silence sat and there, it was not powerful. It was a rumble of roiling discontent, dismay, confusion, and bewilderment. Sometimes, it was rage. I noted a pact of silence, of not telling, among women: Do not tell pregnant women that mothering is hard or that you will be blamed for all things inconvenient or difficult for men, children, and other wild things. We tell other women instead that they glow. We do not tell girls that making art while mothering is next to impossible. Instead, we watch them draw and dance and swirl — and give them music lessons and watercolours and a plethora of brushes.

My mother painted for the first time in 1973. She tells me that she did it with a Q-tip, using a tin of watercolours from her children's stash of art supplies. Both of my brothers and I had been furnished with pastels, paints, inks, and drawing pads, as it was known that art was good for the children. The twelve hard circles of dried compacted pigments had names like Sky Blue, Deep Green, Crimson Red, and Burnt Sienna. She softened the colours with drops of water from a small glass at her side.

Did the Q-tip provide the texture that she wanted, or did she not have time, agency to leave and go find the right paintbrush perhaps a step above our plastic bristles? Was this improvisation a quest to create the right texture on paper, a need to find an instrument just for herself, previously untouched by our play, or was it yet another "make-do" — a denial of self? Why this sudden urge to express something ephemerous, to create something concrete from it and place it into world?

She is ninety now. She remembers clearly and answers.

Her painting was of a man on a bike passing by the gate as she sat on the front porch at our home in Blue Range, Trinidad. A minute, brightly coloured hummingbird hovered just above his head. She had not painted before. "It was just an impulse," she said. Where is the painting?

"I don't know, I was never in one spot long enough to continue anything. It is hard to track anything when you move all the time."

In my mother's case, the married state meant the impulse to create was held down, held back, undernourished. She carried the world and was too busy when a quest for artmaking awoke briefly in her being. "I was the centre of keeping the kids going," she said. It meant that all obvious physical signs of her art disappeared as we left one house and set up in another, over and over again, following her husband's career to Trinidad and back to Canada and the various postings between and around those oceanic moves. I asked

her again what she'd been looking for when she'd picked up that
Q-tip to paint.

"Liberation," she said.

## Advice

I found an essay entitled "How to Be an Artist, According to
Georgia O'Keeffe," written by Alexxa Gotthardt.[1] The painter had
a daily routine, with much time alone in her studio. She wrote once
to a friend, "I was at work before eight — stopped a couple of hours
at noon — then at it again till six — I will be at it again tomorrow."
The essay mentions the efficiencies of ritual and neatness, and the
organization of space. I think the greatest efficiencies lie within the
Single Mother Artist who still manages to write a line of a poem
sometime within a six-month span. And it is a good line. The hard-
est part to learn is to be okay with one line, when there is space for
nothing else. It may be difficult to calm the yearning and not pine
too much for more time and energy; to be okay with the beautiful
phrase, crafted in the mind while sitting/working/feeding/manag-
ing. The most efficient use of the creative impulse, sometimes, is to
harness it, and tell it to wait while you keep self and others alive.
Metro. Boulot. Dodo. Work. Feed. Fall down. Then act in corners
of time. Sometimes, to be efficient, it is best to eat an orange, feel the
sweet nectar drip from your lips and onto your neck, down beneath
your tired clothing and then, for one second, birdlike — look up.

I advise one to carry a notebook at all times — a small one that
does not take up much space on your person or in your thoughts,
because your being is required elsewhere.

I advise one to keep a close eye on doors when sitting on the subway. This public transit state of vigilance is common among most
Black people, many women, and mothers travelling with children

of any age. This positioning allows the self a modicum less anxiety in a public place. And as the train slows to a stop at each station, you can note easily who gets on. It allows one to stay vigilant and yet have a fleeting freedom, when for a moment you must disappear into a phrase.

Write out your worries first in the notebook, I'd say. Spill out all the concerns about food, foyer, and family court. After you've done that and perhaps found a temporary respite, the art will come. It always does. You just don't know if you'll get to the end of your worries before disembarkment at Eglinton Station, where you do mindless work to pay for food, foyer, and family court. Maybe by then you will have written a phrase. If so, it is a good art day. Maybe it is even a beautiful phrase.

Accept long fallow periods. This is also artistic work. You must wait. Until someone stops banging on the door, until the child stops crying, until you can breathe again. Eat. Go outside, if you can. Walk the city streets for a second or two — whatever is available to you — if the children are old enough for you to do this. Otherwise, stay put. During these fallow periods. Dance. Sing. Wait. Hold. Hold. Hold. Until, until. The being rests and builds up inspiration, and courage, and when "all full up," as it feels to me, produces a creative act. One poem. A flourish of an arm.

Oh … and carry a seed. I mean it. Carry a seed in your left hand, or your right. Paint your belly in magnificent colours under your clothes, to help remember who you are. The time will arise again in glorious panache, if only for one second or a few.

The discipline is holding against the pull of distraction that would keep you immobilized. Note how you are held under. Note how you were held back. Note that it is not your failure. Acknowledge the energy expended while also navigating through colonialist structures and the mentalities that embolden them. See how some imagine their own injury as they cause harm, as they try to silence you with their shivering tears. See clearly who might try to shut you down. There are those who would let you drown. Write, dance through to the other side of this knowing. Something lies there. It can be beauty. It could be art. The discipline is kindness to self when none of this is possible. The discipline is forgiving yourself when you cannot do it all and lying down to rest if only for a moment.

Awake even earlier. This is time that no one can tread on. Until they do. It is not the existence of men, children, and other wild things that will kill you. It is expectation and entitlement, a social understanding that you are not a Self and that you must give your All away, even your silence. Otherwise, you are stealing.

Ask your significant people to be holders, protectors of your space. Together, create the structure within which you make your art. If they will not/cannot, find your own way.

Have at least one Jacqueline — the friend who says, "I know your life is shit and you have no time. Do not lose yourself. I want from you one piece a month, for one year, on anything." This friend gives you assignments and then publishes them. "Take yourself seriously," she says. "They won't. Before you leave for the long commute to work, print out these musings. There might be space to edit on the way. Put pen to paper." Sometimes I take a laptop; however, that requires a whole other level of awareness on public transport. Either way, I work in short bursts. I move from metaphor to metaphor. I sip quickly, locate a glorious moment and breathe in. If you can do none of this on some days, listen and watch the others on transit as they move, sleep, think, feel.

Keep everything. Well. Most of it. When you move, place your art in a box. Never let it out of your sight. Sometimes, all you will do is look at it sideways at night, over there on the shelf as you fall into an exhausted slumber. There is power in holding bits of yourself and carrying your own house on your back.

One year, I pulled everything out of that box. Twenty-year-old poems, an unreleased album of songs; clippings of published poems, performances, classes; various bands of my own making and those of others. I pulled strands of myself that lay scattered around the corners of my life on clusters of yellowing paper. I pulled together all of those whispers and brought them forward. Once gathered, they looked like a thing, an identity that I could share as a whole — more than murmurings from a corner of a desk in the dark, more than writing "on the side."

Once we were grown, she did try it again. My mother. Painting. One summer afternoon, this time in suburban Ottawa. I noted that she'd bought some paints, brushes, a couple of small canvases and placed them in a corner of the basement. I understood that to paint, one needed light and a place to set up an easel. The enormous darkened room — filled with cardboard boxes filled with ideas of belonging that we'd dragged from house to house — was not conducive to such things.

## Birdsong

I wander around my Toronto neighbourhood, walking Jazz, my golden, curly haired spaniel-poodle mix, sipping coffee. I then make my way back home, knowing that I've taken care of an important aspect of being. This ritual is part of a long series of artistic acts, so subtle that they are unrecognizable as such from the exterior of self. I know, however, that strands are forming out of ether, and that soon, I will raise my hand, make a fist, and pull them — a sentence, a word, a paragraph, a lifeline — forward into this place.

It is minute choices that determine if a woman lives or dies, whether or not her soul stays entirely her own. Often, we give these moments away or they are stolen and mount into carnivorous years.

We then drag ourselves onward with hearts emptied of blood. We awaken suddenly, fully depleted without art, without breath, with no legacy other than the worldly accomplishments of others.

Even though I have never heard hummingbirds sing, I imagine that they do. I imagine my mother, the painter, racing from colour to colour, sipping the nectars of love and art, moving with wings that flutter so rapidly they are invisible.

# Ancestor

*The thing is, we carry them with us always in these bodies. The Kalinago, the Indians perhaps from Uttar Pradesh, my African perhaps-Ewe self — and the well-named Europeans.*

All of my dolls were named Elizabeth, the name of my mother's grandmother, a woman I'd never met. Elizabeth, Elizabeth, Elizabeth, Elizabeth, and Elizabeth. I called her into the present with my child voice. I called her in as I said the name to each blond-and-pink plastic shell of a body. She was missing from me and I wanted her close.

One day, my elder brother gathered up all my dolls from their scattered corners of our most recent home. The Calypso Road March that year, "Sixty-Seven" by Lord Kitchener, spoke about how much fun one could have. Outside the two-storey building on Senior Street, in the neighbourhood of Diego Martin, my brother carefully lined up the dolls on the first few steps of the stairs leading to the apartment above. He then took aim and shot them each in the head and chest with his new pellet gun. I did not see the event, only the bloodless aftermath of pink plastic bodies strewn around the stones and scrappy grass. I tearfully collected my plastic babies, peeking sideways at my brother in confusion and horror. I desperately asked my mother, Why? I might as well have asked, Why History?

It was as if, in these child actions, we inhabited tales that lived in our bones — an ancestor, an old war — and gave them life. My brother, an intuitive, as all children are, enacted what had happened next to the Kalinago and Taino of the islands under European hands in the 1400s. He then unwittingly shot the colonizer, over and over and over again.

There is no photo of our Elizabeth. She was Kalinago. The name Elizabeth was a Protestant imposition. We learned in school that the Caribs of the Caribbean islands were extinct, the convenience of lands emptied of people and there for the taking. This makes no sense. Elizabeth's face comes through in the few photos of her daughter, my grandmother Nita (Angela). The original peoples of the Americas still live in the Trinidad village of Lopinot, on Dominica, and throughout the islands. They also live on in my mother's face and eyes, and in the bodies and blood of my family.

Aren't we all a gathering of origin stories, held in memories, bodies, and faces? My family evolved from a plethora of lineages and cannot compute within the fractions and percentages of a genealogy database. It exists in story. Even so, I decide to look beyond and behind the family's collective memory. And because most of us mostly look like descendants of the continent of Africa, I begin here. I signed up for a class at the Toronto Public Library North York Branch. Genealogist Pooran Bridgelal's "Introduction to Tracing Your African Heritage in the British West Indies" was held in a small meeting room on the second floor. Fifteen seekers, mostly women of Black Caribbean origin, holding the mixed shades of multiple heritages common in the Caribbean sat around the tables. We held our notebooks, pens, and the expectant faces of those with a history of absence. Other genealogy courses that I'd come across before this one had not been for us. They allowed people of European heritage to find distant kin in Ireland and England, and did not touch the complex histories of those with enslaved ancestors, stolen names and land, transatlantic voyages forced and otherwise, and multiple heritages from all the continents and races of the world. Tracing family histories in what was called the British West Indies is specific and complex.

Our African presence in the Americas began in the 1400s, 1492 or so. Our names are long gone. Untraceable. Because of what is euphemistically called the Middle Passage, the route of the Slave Trade from Europe to Africa to the Americas, where the kidnapped Africans were walked around the forgetting tree and unnamed, there is little to follow. Our original names and languages do not sit in our mouths. Some clues sit in archives in England or Scotland, on ships' rosters or among lists of property bought, sold, and insured in case of damage or drowning during the shipping process. In Trinidad, the Red House, a holder of documents and records of our pasts, burned down and was rebuilt without many of them.

I could travel abroad, try to find such documents. Since so much has disappeared, disappearance itself is a presence. I decide instead to travel inwards. I will hold this nameless absence in my hands.

•

This is the hidden history we've come from. I was raised somewhat innocent, exposed to a minimum of ugliness, although that was soon to come in, fast and furious. I was a private-schooled doctor's daughter, far in experience from the enslaved peoples who exist in my family's very bones, skin, and hair. My parents were respectable. Their parents were respectable. My grandmothers did embroidery and taught European classical piano. Both grandfathers were school principals and choirmasters. So, I come by this sound and word-smithing business rightly.

Until I embraced this (the writing), however, I lived with silences. Old patterns live deep. Centuries-old habits can be whipped into flesh, screams, and fear held mute over eons become a habit. When there has always been retribution for the act of speaking, one learns to be still. This ability served me well for many years until it did not. Stillness began to choke me. My history included beings who were kidnapped, sold, and resold; it included European "explorers" and African "traders" in human flesh; it included forced travels — continent to island, island to island, plantation to plantation. Plantation is a sweet word that holds echoes of sunlight and white-pillared homes rather than visions of torture fields and forced work camps. I cannot settle and be still with such memories because my body remembers, even if my mind cannot. I realized if I did not write, my silence might slay me.

Many people of European descent don't want to hear this. Many people of African descent don't want to remember. There are those of us descended from both who have no choice but to remember, as the alternative is to be faceless. It is the job of poets and songwriters to repeat what dwells within us, to bring it forth, drag it up by the heels like a newborn from the rich, dark, moist earth of the unconscious and let it ring. The memory cannot lie locked in guilt or shame's chest. We must crack it open with hammers of flesh, with dreams and mirrors. I know the names of the Africans, someplace in my being. I speak their names with the unheard language of the heart, and I lift my arm in a gesture of greeting.

However, I only know what I know. And so, to summon those ancestors more clearly, I call for a different kind of assistance.

At a workshop with Heloisa Porto, a local shaman, originally from Brazil, I "see" that a paternal African ancestor who was Christianized refused to let me pass or tell me what he knew of those who came before him. The ones behind him, all men, stood up and came forward. I asked where the women were. The women rose from behind the men and said, we have always been here, we just have a different role. I did not fully understand my vision. "You need to speak with Malidoma," said Heloisa.

My first meeting with Malidoma Somé was in Roncesvalles Village, a predominantly Polish neighbourhood in Toronto. The esteemed shaman, academic, and teacher, until his death in 2021, had flown regularly between North America and his village in Burkina Faso, bringing teachings and wisdom from his people, the Dagara, to the minds of "the West." This intermediary role between cultures was predicted by his elders. His name means, "be friends with the stranger/enemy." At this point, as a being raised in the Americas, I am definitely of "the West," and I gathered that Malidoma could help explain my vision and draw linkages between my worlds.

It is a wintry November day and I stand on the porch of a large Victorian-style three-storey dwelling. Around me, the trees are bare, the light is grey, the day holds still, like my breath. I exhale and press the ringer. A white woman in her mid-fifties opens the door. This is Leslie Fell, a local spiritual leader and, I learn later, a student of the man with whom I've come to consult. She is fit, white-haired, wears a long skirt. She leads me into the living room. I sit on a wooden chair and wait. For quite some time. Then, Malidoma Somé enters the room. He is bespectacled and robed, at once regal and humble. We both sit on the floor. I turn on my recording device.

I tell him what I saw during Heloisa's workshop. Yes, he says. That's them. Ancestors coming forth. What they called themselves has disappeared. I imagine they called themselves "the people," as other groups do. Anishinaabe, Habesha.

I tell Malidoma that sometimes I find deep ancestral links in ordinary places. Once at a workplace, I recognized a colleague from Ghana as a medicine man. I greeted him respectfully as such. The man, a sociologist by all available reckoning, had looked at me startled. He'd been hiding in plain sight in this culture, wearing ordinariness as a kind of spiritual camouflage. We talked of my work. He said little of his, and then he offered me this: "You are from the Ewe people, like me. I can see it in your face."

I also say I found the Africans within me when I learned to dance the Orixás in Brazil. The body is a university. It carries eons. You just need to learn its vocabulary. There are direct messages from the past in the flourish of an arm.

I say that my cousin Louis somehow found his way back to a Blizzard who bought himself out of slavery and whose son, another Blizzard, became a shipbuilder, who begat another shipbuilder who begat a ship's captain (the brother of a Canadian Blizzard) who begat Eggerton (my grandfather) who married Engracia. Was Blizzard a French name or an English name? Depends on how you say it.

Malidoma listens. His deep black eyes hold a light that is both fierce and gentle. He nods in understanding. He confirms that family stories and experiences, my dreams and memories, even unwritten, indeed transmit history. "You have been able to formulate the dilemma of multiplicity within unity," he says, and then, "this is the breakdown of a deep story that could come out in the form of a book." And so, comforted and emboldened I call my other ancestors in as well.

•

Centuries after the wholesale kidnapping of people from Africa, my Indian ancestors were deposited on the island of Saint Vincent, between 1861 and 1886.

Slavery officially ended in Saint Vincent on August 1, 1834. At this point, many formerly enslaved Africans refused to continue the brutal labour of cutting and processing sugar cane. Many options to fill this role were considered. Chinese people were a considered import. However, the cost of one shipment of humans from so far away was exorbitant. Poor whites from Barbados were considered an option. Eventually, deals were made with the government of India and European agents of Saint Vincent. Indians were contracted for five or ten years, for a few pence a day and some supplies of sugar, rum, and molasses. After five years, workers could receive a plot of land. After ten, one could get free passage back to India.

In "Arrival of Indians in St. Vincent," historian Dr. Arnold Thomas notes that Governor Francis Hinds did not support the strategic initiative to bring people from India for what he termed "mitigated slavery." Firstly, it would have underbid free Blacks in the paid labour market and would certainly produce "racial animosity"[1] — the results of which we often witness today. The latter economic strategy was pursued. A few Indians from Saint Vincent migrated to Trinidad, among them my people. Somewhere between 1845 and 1917, 143,939 Indians were also imported directly to Trinidad. I use that word with intention — their bodies were fuel for the sugar industry that fed palates and pocketbooks, building the wealth of Europe.

I cannot follow these ancestors of mine very far back. Their names disappeared early on when they were renamed. The habit at the time was to impose the surname of the European landholder (I say this specifically, the holder of land that was not his, or shall I be more specific: land thieves) on the people brought to work there. In my family story, my mother tells me their names may have disappeared under Jean LaBorde, a French priest who indentured them. We really don't know. She once met a man from India who looked like her father. He told her he was from Uttar Pradesh. Now, we imagine, perhaps we also come from there.

In 1999, I returned to the library for another course by Pooran Bridgelal called "Introduction to Tracing Your Indian Heritage in the British West Indies." The room was filled with those who looked overtly Indian, and those like me, clearly of African origin. We listened, took notes, asked a multitude of questions. Along with the many books and websites he gave us, he suggested a visit to the archives at the Mormon Centre. Starting in the late 1800s, the Mormon Church has documented and stored marriages, births, baptisms, and deaths of people around the world. They believe that people can be baptized by proxy in the Mormon Church as long as they know their names and lineage, with or without their permission, alive or dead. This included Catholic and Anglican parishes on small Caribbean islands. They were very thorough in their pursuit of salvation for all. The information, originally collected on paper notecards, has been microfiched and digitized. It is stored in the church's FamilySearch Centers around the world. Strange and incredibly useful.

My travel to the Church of Jesus Christ of Latter-Day Saints in the suburbs of Toronto was an hour-and-a-half trek by a combination of subway and buses. I disembarked from my final bus ride and crossed a half-empty parking lot to the east door of the building. I rang the bell. I circled, I checked my watch. I waited. Tried again. I thought about the beliefs of the Mormons, that marriage is for life and that they were determined to keep records and hold people together in the afterlife. I wondered how many divorced people would be happy with that. I journeyed through these thoughts, ringing the doorbell periodically until thirty-five minutes later, a small white woman opened the door. She smiled and showed me into a dark cave of a room. Here were small white boxes of micro-fiches stored by island and by year. I started in Saint Vincent and the first-known family story of my mother's paternal people, the LaBordes. I fumbled with the clunky microfiche machines, sliding strands of film into slots so that the information could be magni-fied and projected onto a screen. After an hour, I found my first LaBorde, first name Jean.

Jean LaBorde was from France and was listed as a mariner, a title I imagine is code for slaver on a slave ship. I kept digging, or should I say sliding. I found bits and pieces of scattered information, unusual names strung together that continued into my generation:

> *Jean LaBorde — mariner arrived in St. Vincent in 1771. He fathered Maximus.*

> *Maximus + Mary Francis LaBorde had Harriet and Edward.*

> *Edward + Georgina LaBorde had Horatio William.*

> *1831: Horatio William + Catherine LaBorde had John Eustace.*

> *1904: John Eustace + Edith Henrietta LaBorde had Eustace Horacio.*

> *Eustace Horacio is my mother's father. They called him Rio (pronounced Ryo) for short.*

I wrote all this in a notebook with my child-self, in my best handwriting, using a flat-nibbed refillable ink pen. "Italics," my peers and I called it. As good British subjects at Bishop Anstey

Private School, Trinidad, in the 1960s and '70s, we were all trained in calligraphy. This habit of good penmanship has mostly disappeared from me. It comes forth through my hand when information is poignant or needs care.

•

My parents' bookshelves were well stocked with a preponderance of self-published books by Trinidadians seeking to trace their family trees. We are all hungry for ourselves; however, few of these books lead the seekers/authors directly to Africa, India, or to the Indigenous of the Caribbean islands (or China for that matter, another significant yet smaller source of the island's population). I can trace any European ancestor back to the 16th century. Because the names belong somewhere, they have been written down. The Europeans in my chart are more easily tracked than the unnamed or misnamed. I quiz my mother and father on our family tree. I make circles and lines tracking who begat who, going backwards for four generations. The Scots are ever present in the Caribbean and are everywhere in my chart — the Davidsons on one side, the Baileys, Callenders, and Hinksons on the other. There are a few Spaniards.

In Paul Crooks's *A Tree Without Roots*,[2] he references a list of thousands of Scots who lived on the Caribbean islands between 1707 and 1857. They are documented by name, island, date, occupation, and so on. The first wave of Scots transferred to the islands in 1654[3] were the disposable ones — prisoners of war, felons, or Covenanters (political undesirables, Crooks calls them) — and were the start of a stream of Scots sold to the English as indentured servants, or bond servants. The English also bought Irish political prisoners, prisoners of war, and ordinary citizens kidnapped by slaver gangs[4] who they enslaved on the islands.

The European names are easy to follow. And there is a coat of arms for every one of the European names that we carry. These identifiers of caste and kin were developed in Europe's middle ages and were worn on the armour and shields of warriors during battle and tournaments. The coat of arms for my paternal family name, Blizzard, includes a shield of silver with a black chevron and three blue crosses moline. The crest above the shield and helmet depicts a white female hand with a bracelet around her wrist. The maternal name Callender is Scottish. The shield is black and gold, a sash from left to right, six billets of wood. The crest above this helmet is of a white male cubit arm holding a billet. It has a motto in Latin: *Bene Ego Volo* — "I mean well." Hmmm, say that to the Taino.

We carry these European names like knapsacks. They are ours; they are how we call ourselves. They are the languages that we speak. English. Spanish. French. Portuguese. Blizzard, Engracia, Bailey, Davidson, John, Elizabeth, Callender, Rio, LaBorde. My uncle Chee-Wah Ng joined in later — a modern day migration of choice. He knew all of his names.

•

Malidoma Somé gathers his energies and his robes, breathes in, sits, closes his eyes. Outside, the November light drifts through the living room window. I see that this work drains him. His expression is very serious. I'm anxious about what he might say about my inquiry, my quest. I wonder if he thinks we, the often-rootless Black peoples of the Americas, with our multitude of origins, seem needy to him. Perhaps he is just tired. He gathers in his hands a collection of stones, shells, bottle caps, and gems. He breathes out and throws the objects onto the large square of coloured fabric laid out between us. The objects clatter, roll, then stop. They shimmer in the grey light that seeps through the bay window behind us. He observes the display and divines the following:

> When you are a representation of multiplicity, you cannot pick one and by so doing exclude others. This discrimination fosters adjacent problems that one piece that you have picked cannot resolve. All need to be together for a sense of wholeness. It is what is closest to truth. You cannot be dwelling on this without looking at history, how an individual journey has meant taking on various legacies and how environment, geography is also contributing to this complexity. We live in a complex world radically different from ancient tribal life that was very simple. So, perhaps what the ancestors are making reference to when they say you are inching slowly home, it is to a place where integration and reconciliation between various departments of wisdom come together to form a unity.

Malidoma is an ancestor now. He has left this plane. I can call him in. I had lots of practice with my dolls. Malidoma. Malidoma. Malidoma Somé. From him I understand that the exact percentage of which DNA of each ethnicity is not the point. Our bloods mingle in microscopic unions. In this cellular dance, we are pulled into being, along with blindness, our whips and slaughters, our earth and our seas. "Over there," he had said to me, waving above his head, "the ancestors, they all get along."

*Seselelame. I have never used this word in a sentence and yet it explains how I walk between worlds. A bodily way of knowing, navigating psychic space and spiritual geographies.*

# Trains and Laundromats

t was while writing a poem at 5:00 a.m. on the first morning in my new apartment at 87 Keele Street that I first noted the scent of death. The early morning spring breeze reeked of fear and blood. My nasal passages were assaulted, my eyes crinkled against this new truth. I had recently returned to vegetarianism after a short stint at age five and was again sensitive to the scent of flesh, alive or dead. Unwittingly, I'd just moved downwind of an abattoir.

This was my second home in Toronto. And except for that early morning discovery, it was generally a good one. It was a few steps from Keele subway station. There was a laundromat at the southeast corner of the intersection at Bloor. A second corner held stone pillars and a side entrance to the forested urban swath of High Park. On the northwest corner was a home for the elderly, and at the fourth corner stood the gas station, which was not of any use to me as I was transit bound. Right next to the gas station was a small strip mall with a sushi place that, in either an auspicious act or an omen, put mayonnaise on everything. Subway stops across the city were to become my physical and emotional cornerstones as I perched in new apartments and rooms in houses up and down the Bloor line over the next thirty years.

My first home had been in Toronto's East End. Coxwell Station. I'd often wondered: Who was Keele? What was a Coxwell? I've since found out; however, if I give that space and exploration right now, I shut down my own story. Here is what I will say instead. A five-minute walk from Coxwell Station was Milverton Boulevard, a tree-lined street where leaves rustled above my head, blessing me as I walked home late at night from my waitressing job. I was searching for a way forward in life beyond the routines and strictures of schooling in science and fashion. And it was here, in the East End, that I stumbled into the martial art of tai chi and studied it for the next twenty years. It was here at the Big Carrot health food store that I found attractive and convincing vegetarians. By the time I moved across town to Keele Station, I'd dropped beef, chicken, fish, and eventually pork.

At the time, I was also reading Pablo Neruda's *Residence on Earth* almost exclusively. Embedded among the sensual images and luscious words was the notion of repeated leavings and returns. The line "no duerme nadie en / por el mundo — out in the world / no one sleeps" spoke to me. I clung to those words as one might to a crucial message from a benevolent guide. And so, in my city, I wandered nocturnally through the terrain of dreams, ideas, and words. I made night forays to Lee's Palace, south on Spadina Avenue to the El Mocambo, and down to Queen Street's Cameron House, where sculptured giant ants clung to its awning. I carried a notebook, watching, listening, noting, pulling meaning and directions for my heart, quests for grace. One could say, in the movement from here to there, that suspended place of motion, I would find a hovering solace in intracity underground voyages. I enjoyed the repeated emergence, climbing steps up into the daylight or the fresh night air again and again, eternally renewed. I felt the subway stops become part of my psyche. As the deer and coyote developed tracks by taking the same route day after day, through patches of forest in the urban wilds of High Park, invisible grooves through the city created neural pathways in my brain.

Built in 1954, the Toronto subway was initially one north–south line. It never evolved much beyond two lines, one an extended *U* with flappy arms and the other an east-to-west corridor across the city, from suburb to suburb. It later grew little flailing shoots in the form of the six-stop line through Scarborough in the east, the five-stop Sheppard Line, and another extension that led up to and then past York University. And more recently, laid overtop like a garland, a four-stop train to the airport. I retained a loyalty to the east–west line, however. At last count, I'd changed homes to spots up and down that line eleven times.

Even as the trains held me, however, I noted a dis-ease with their names embedded in my language as I crossed the city, names thought or repeated out loud daily as I moved through space. The stations were named for a series of would-be Euro-kings: Coxwell, Broadview, Chester, Dundas, Keele, Jane. Perhaps one Euro-queen. In *The Address Book*, Deirdre Mask says, "The state can literally put words in your mouth."[1] I wondered if these words on my tongue might have misinformed or undermined my younger self. I wonder if repeating those names confirmed the histories of would-be conquerors of those like me and ensured that mine remained less visible, even to myself.

I continued to counter-whisper Neruda's "Furies and Sorrows," in Spanish and then English:

> That's the way life is,
>> you, run among the leaves and a belt
>> of yellow metal,
> while the mist of the station corrodes the stones.[2]

## Home 3/11

Sometime after Coxwell and Keele, I made a one-year stop to live at Christie Station. On the south side of Bloor is a four-storey red brick apartment building. Here I took a room in the home of a woman, let's call her Barb. We were not roommates, as it was abundantly clear that I was not welcome in the dining room, in the living room where she inexplicably did meditation yoga while watching television at full volume, or in the kitchen. My room was at the entry. I skulked between my room, short visits to the kitchen for tea, and the bathroom, with brief forays into the dining room to eat. I slept on the floor, on a futon, surrounded by books and guitars.

While living at Christie Station (the street was named by a wealthy merchant after his wife, Christy with a *y*, in 1835), in a back lane behind an ice cream shop one July in the 1980s, I stumbled upon a noisy and joyful gathering. The rehearsal for Caribana by a Brazilian music group was led by Bruce and Eliane Jones. It was a confusing clatter of percussion instruments, guitars, and voice. A small girl was doing a strange rhythm with her feet and hips. I'd never seen any of this before. Musician Rodrigo Chavez saw my confusion and broke it down for me. Feet do this, he counted out, "Tah ka taaa, Tah ka taaa" and showed me the rhythm with his feet. I was taken in by something resonant embedded in the rhythm and the movement. This musical happening provided me with an unexpected anchor for the next few decades — songlines through treacherous terrain.

## Home 5/11

Next stop: Sherbourne Station. My new home was in a soon-to-be condemned house steps from the intersection of Sherbourne and

Bloor. The four-storey Victorian was filled with actors and musicians. It also housed a worm farm in the basement. The street and later subway station had been named by Samuel Ridout in 1845 after Sherborne (different spelling), his birthplace in Dorset, England.

By this time, I'd discovered another musical connection, having stumbled onto a drumming circle in High Park, where a sea of colourfully dressed would-be hippie children of all nations played djembes. A few souls gyrated and spun in the centre of the circle. My oven in the ground-floor apartment was only ever used for tightening the goat skins of the drums. At 1:30 every Sunday afternoon, I'd set it to 230 degrees Celsius (who is Celsius?). At 2:00 p.m., Joseph Ashong, Michael Vertolli, and Jesse Cook would arrive. They would pull up chairs, open the oven door, and lean their djembes into the heat. I played a rough and perhaps insulting approximation of a djun djun — a two-headed metal surdo with fibreglass heads. I'd turned it on its side and screwed a silver cowbell to one end. No heating was required, as I tightened it with a metal key. Under Joseph's tutelage, we developed a small repertoire of Ghanaian rhythms. We called ourselves Enijé Ensemble and had our band name printed across the back of bright yellow T-shirts. The old house shook for three hours each week as we practised. No one seemed to mind. I engaged in a series of such gatherings, strange, foreign, urban culture collaborations in an attempt to perhaps feel a part of something, home-like.

When I saw *Télésculpture* by conceptual artist Panayiotis Vassilakis (Takis) in the Musée d'art contemporain de Montréal, it spoke to me instantly. It worked with invisible magnetic forces. Kinetic art, it was called. It used magnetism to suspend forms in space. A sculpture of both stasis and movement. A moment and eons captured in one structure. I was entranced by the metal cones, a white sphere, and apparent weightlessness. I know that place of in-between made manifest in a visible form. It validated me somehow.

When you are always "foreign," you don't expect belonging and can remain in a suspended, ungrounded searching state. You move differently in the world, watching for the lay of the land to shift under your feet. It's not that I found moving easy, I just never expected to stay still, which in itself is a very specific state — of non-staying. You hold yourself aloft and are ready to go around the perceptions of others, to find a different route or to disconnect and move to another plane, where that particular pain does not sit. You hover in a timeline that is more reasonable, listening for directions, maps that make more sense. You are most at home in laundromats and moving trains. Both locations provide sound, motion, and womb-like comfort for a small fee.

You come boundaried and carry a space within you that is not of place, which sets up camp and decamps almost as easily. You recall the forced decampments when either you or all your friends and community were transferred, scattered across the country following the requirements of the military father. You understand precarity and have a readiness to flee that would terrify lovers. The training of movement runs deep. This pattern stayed in my nervous system far beyond the time of its usefulness.

## Home 10/11

Later, I lived for one year on Colbeck Street, near Jane Station, named by Scottish real estate developer James Barr in the early 1900s. Barr named developments after family members — Jane was his wife. I lived here with two roommates in a three-storey, five-bedroom behemoth, a former rooming house that had been reclaimed as a home. I had a studio for writing and music in the fourth bedroom. I read and wrote poetry, some of which became lyrics for my songs that I eventually recorded. And like many other artists in literature, film, and music around the world, from Puerto Rican composer Awilda Villarini to pop band the Tragically Hip, strains of Neruda made their way into my music:

"In the depths of our hearts, we are together in a summer of tigers. Desperate furies and sorrows are gone in some summer place," I wrote.

The furies and sorrows were not gone. I moved one stop east to Runnymede Station and continued to make a clusterfuck of bad choices. Next stop was Dundas West, where for the following fifteen years, like a homing pigeon who does not learn well, I lived at spots five to fifteen minutes away from this central locus, named after a man who vehemently contested the abolition of the enslavement of people who looked exactly like me.

The subway cars are not always places of hiding. The seeming nest underground has always held threat for some, and this has only become more obvious due to recent stabbings. Nestled on red fabric and up against the metal corner of a subway car on the north–south line to Sheppard Station, I was busy noting in my notebook on the way to a job interview. I knew there was little money in poetry, songs, waitressing, temping, and promotion-less government positions, and was hoping to become director of a branch of an after-school program. I was charged, hopeful, happy, and of course, writing. A South Asian Caribbean man, long wavy hair, spotted me and started to scream racial epithets at me. His heavy Guyanese accent (or was it Trini?) and instability revealed simultaneously. I tried to avoid any eye contact; however, he came closer. I sank into my seat, all assurance and preparation for the coming interview gone. A medium-build white man — leather jacket, brown hair, moustache, shades — approached me as well.

"Do you want some help?" he asked. Yes, I nodded.

He turned to the man, pulled out a badge, showed it to my tormenter and told him to get off the car or he'd be arrested. A bit of shoving back and forth. My tormentor shuffled off at the next stop. The Columbo-like saviour turned to me and said, "This is not a real police badge, but I carry it around and it helps a lot." He smiled, shrugged, and got off at the next stop. I sat there, adrenalin still rushing through my body. I wished for someone to acknowledge what had just occurred, to ask me if I was okay, touch my hand. Instead, people on the subway car sat immobile, watching my distress. Slowly, tears began to leak from the corners of my eyes. My shoulders drooped as I realized my extreme aloneness in the presence of so many. The apathy, inaction, and refusal of care in that subway car had more impact on me than the incident itself. I, too, got off at the following stop and re-entered the next train filled with a different group of strangers who had witnessed nothing.

A moment of such invisibility can create an exile from self, confirming my strange legacy of restlessness. This is not so easily overcome by the occasional strand of comprehension — a breath of wisdom — or strange white man with a brown leather coat and a fake badge, or by running to nest in a new place.

Debra Thompson captures this home-in-motion tendency in *The Long Road Home: On Blackness and Belonging*: "Paradoxically, mobility and constraint exist in tandem; it's entirely possible to be homeward bound and yet bound by a peculiar sense of home."[3] I know that now as I chose to live at hubs on a thirty-year subway ride up and down the east–west line. I would descend into a potentially nurturing darkness and repeatedly climb up into the sunlight. At these crossroads of the city, I could meet four corners, four ways, four directions. Even as I repeated the names of various downpressors with each stop, these intersections were places of overlap where multiple wisdoms might meet.

At the Musée d'art contemporain de Montréal in 2022, I saw for the first time the work of artist Firelei Báez of the Dominican

Republic. She'd painted Ciguapa, an imaginary Dominican figure — a trickster with long hair covering her naked body. In the painting at the Musée d'art contemporain de Montréal, Ciguapa is crouched in front of a page from an atlas entitled *Terra Nova*. There is a Spanish flag and other symbols of colonial ideologies and practices. Ciguapa is superimposed on the map, her hair bundled and adorned with leaves and flowers. Báez disrupts the colonial map with visual tales, visceral pathways. Histories become compressed, multi-dimensional, physical, clear, acknowledged.

I recall from the time of childhood in the Caribbean another way of stating space. We lived on Hermitage Road, Port of Spain, Trinidad (I won't unpack "Port of Spain" or even "Trinidad" for that matter, here and now). The word "hermitage" felt lovely on the tongue, giving images of something quaint — perhaps a grassy knoll that I'd read about in books not written in the Caribbean, where sat perhaps a miniscule house or a monk near a cave. My family had lived among other lovely names like Blue Range, Petit Valley, La Puerta Avenue. Sometimes words can be blue, small, door-like openings.

Today I have circled back to live near Keele Station. Even as it is named for William Conway Keele, a Junction-area landowner, this is my third landing at this location. Three times lucky. No? After years of sinking and emergence, I arrive right back where I began. Maybe this is the opening that I must now walk through. I do different work now — this still involves significant noting in notebooks. I still write poems. There is still a laundromat on the corner. It glitters with fluorescent lighting. It looks like a place where one might be served tea. There is still a place for the elderly on another corner, the pillared entrance to High Park on a third, and yes, there is still a gas station. I live a few blocks north now. My window faces the back end of the city, away from the beacon green of High Park. It is 4:00 a.m. I'm thinking of the right word to place in a phrase.

I know now that words keep me from exile. A mall sits where the abattoir once was. I hear that one or two slaughtering floors remain there, tucked into the concrete landscape. They no longer smell. I still do not eat meat.

# Cooking with Esteban, and Other Adventures in Salvador, Bahia

I chose men who could pitch a tent, cook a meal over an open fire, stack logs, place the furniture and books and magazines just so ... and make a wicked curry. A man who knew that there was a special pasta pot with a built-in steel colander. The type of man who could take me to a kitchen store and tell me what kind of frying pan I need in my household in order for him to make proper pancakes — not the giant steel wok with the flattened base that I usually used. A man who knew of the existence of a muddler and tested the weight-in-hand of a good quality vegetable peeler. A man who could show up unannounced with a packed cooler and say, "Let's go."

I grew up in household with a father who wouldn't lift a finger. At age eighty-seven, he deigned to make himself a cup of tea, while my mother was briefly hospitalized. Upon her recovery and return home, he immediately stated, "Merle. Tea."

I always thought that I was choosing differently, and yet, it was always revealed eventually, that beneath their claims of "I love to cook" lay their wish for me to rule the kitchen, to heal, feed, clean, encourage, and carry them. Well, except for Esteban, that is. We were never lovers, but I swear he was the most influential man in my life.

> *Dois de Julho, Salvador, Bahia, Brazil, is a barely middle-class neighbourhood interspersed with pockets of ruin. The people here are Black, brown, mixed race — they all look like me. During the day, the cobblestone lanes are filled with cashew, fish, fruit, and vegetable stalls. Cars, pedestrians, and carts negotiate the crowded streets. At night, the stalls disappear. Six of us share a four-storey apartment here during the Afro-Brazilian Orixá movement dance intensive. We enter the apartment for the first time and look around. Esteban, part-time Mariachi musician, part-time Brazilian dance instructor from Tucson, Arizona, points to the walls of our new home, which open up a few feet from the ceiling onto a backyard full of banana trees. "The criminals here must be pretty lazy," he says. I make a note to lock my suitcase and decide to listen to everything he says.*

In my twenties, the oven in my ground-floor apartment was only ever used with its door wide open. My bandmates and I would lean the goat skin heads of our djembes into the heat, tuning them in preparation for our rehearsals of Ghanaian rhythms. Later, during my time as a wife, I was still unclear about the regular use of the oven and other kitchen phenomena. As a young girl, I'd hovered around my mother, in a series of kitchens in a series of homes, witnessing as she managed all meals, along with her own job as a nurse and the schedules of three children. She managed by turning, grabbing ingredients, mixing, moving at the speed of light. Not much time for teaching.

"It's good, but it's not meat," the husband would say jokingly at my detailed casserole presentation. The comment only further discouraged me, as I'd seen so much of another side of cooking: stress, expectation, the relentlessness of three meals a day for years and years. By age eighty-five my mother stopped completely and would only warm up the occasional frozen dinner for herself and my then-ailing father.

•

At sixteen I stood at the kitchen stove of the family's latest home. The permanent married quarters or PMQs for officers of Canadian Forces Base North Bay sat together along a crescent road. The houses were all covered with identical white siding. Concrete steps led up to small concrete porches and screen doors. It was a Northern Ontario summer. A crosswind blew through the front screen, into the kitchen, and out the back door to the shared courtyard. I was being magnanimous, even if uninformed, and I thought I'd help out by making, of all things, a cheese sauce. This I planned to pour onto something else. What that something else might be, I wasn't too sure. I dropped a chunk of cheddar in a saucepan and watched it begin to melt. I became confused when it just bubbled and fried. I asked my mother, what was wrong with the sauce, and she looked at me with what I interpreted as disdain. "What!" I said. "You never showed me anything!" I surmised that I was supposed to just know, to have picked up this kitchen business somehow. However, among the adolescent chaos of a transatlantic move and negotiating the third of my five high schools, I had been somewhat distracted and had not taken in the required feminine skills by osmosis.

I have no kitchen memories from early childhood, no memories of gathering ingredients, of measuring cups of flour and pouring them into a bowl and stirring with Mum (certainly not with Dad). In our constantly new locations, there were no joyful cooking gatherings of women, of loving aunties or grannies. Just one exhausted mother in a strange kitchen-type isolation. My mother has some memories of cooking with her mother who died when my mother was twelve years old. As their father had died seven years earlier, my mother and her siblings became orphans. With two younger siblings to care for, and with some help from her grandmother, she figured out this kitchen business and became good at it. Brilliant even. I recall her scrambling together magical meals out of disparate ingredients. Pelau, curried beef, buljol, bacon and eggs. She made brilliant black cake.

> *In Bahia, we've been told that everyone attends Lavagem do Bonfim, the annual six-kilometre pilgrimage from Cidade Baixa to Igreja do Bonfim, and that everyone wears white. Esteban and I go shopping in Pelourinho, the city centre. Pastel-coloured seventeeth-century buildings housing small shops line the undulating streets. On the narrow sidewalks, vendors sell water, necklaces, maps, purses, paintings, jewellery. There are roaming bands of drummers. I spot a beautiful white dress hanging in a glass window. "Try it on," says Esteban. Incredulous, I look at him skeptically. "I was raised by women," he says. "I know how to wait." I try on dresses, T-shirts, bracelets, earrings, sandals.*

•

"I'm neutral about cooking" says one friend. No woman says this out loud. It is as sacrilegious as saying pregnancy is a slog, motherhood is hard work, or that you don't like wearing heels. Less than womanly. Unfeminine.

"But you gotta eat," she laughs. "I make great meals a few times a week. It takes up a lot of my time — thinking, planning, shopping, prepping — cooking. I'd rather drink shakes. Even my siblings don't know this. I just recently stopped cooking the turkey for family gatherings. I no longer eat turkey and certainly don't want to stick my hand up inside one. They were pissed because we still gather at my house, but if they want turkey, they have to make it themselves and bring it," she says, laughing. "One day I'll be a liquidarian," she states.

Another friend reveals that she resentfully slams the pots around as she creates two separate meals. One for herself — a pescatarian — and another for husband and children — a brisket of some sort.

It is curious how we breathe in unspoken patterns from our family environment. One must move often. The kitchen is a hostile and lonely place. Perhaps, the pattern of moving every two years as a child also influenced me. It was certainly a pattern that followed me into adult life. I continued to change the location of my home as an adult, whether I needed to or not.

*The two-hour bus ride back home is extended when a police motorcycle turns in front of the bus and forces it to stop. Out the window, I see police guns raised at three Black boys, spread-eagled against a concrete wall, their shabby knapsacks on the sidewalk.*

*The locals stand up and strain to look. The Canadians look, too, but stay seated. Eyes down,*

*Esteban is still — even when the police enter the bus to look for another one of the kids. I try to follow suit, but I'm curious. I watch the watchers. When we are finally moving again, I ask Esteban why he did not look up.*

*"I'm Mexican in America," he says. "I've seen enough of that. Where I live, we Latinos and Blacks are not well-treated by the cops."*

*"Where exactly do you live?"*

*"I've always lived in poor neighbourhoods," he explains. He smiles at me, then adds for effect: "When people escape from prison nearby, they hide in our yard." I'm laughing now.*

*"How do you know they're in your yard?" I ask.*

*"Well, the helicopters overhead have searchlights, so when we see them, we just stay inside until they go away." He watches me for response. My world of gluten-free bakeries and art galleries in Toronto's Junction district is far from this world. He knows this. Smiles.*

•

Back home in Canada, the systemic stuff looked a bit different. It was at times a seemingly passive statement. "It's too hard to be the ally of a Black woman," someone once informed me. And then qualified the statement with *"your* kind of Black woman." Which made me wonder, what kind is that? A tall one? A beautiful one? A writerly one? A live one? Whiteness as weapon. I'm so tired.

Back home, the men that I chose said they wanted Woman, but it seemed they actually wanted Mother: someone to fill in the missing spots where they had not been held; to do the work that they did not wish to take on. Someone to lean far too heavily upon. Perhaps they said, "I love to cook," just long enough to hook me. And I chose to believe it. Perhaps they wanted someone to take over where Mother had never been in the first place.

*Some days after dance class, Esteban and I wander through the former slave market, Praça da Sé to Romã, the vegetarian restaurant where many of the dancers meet. The machine-gunned military are on every corner, to protect the tourists, most of whom don't look like either of us.*

*Some evenings after dance class, Esteban and I make dinner. Spaghetti mostly. The tomato sauce comes in an aluminum bag. Sometimes we add onions. We stir in some weird, soft Brazilian cheese. Sometimes after dinner, we have dessert. Maybe a guava. Sometimes a mango. He slices bits of ripe fruit and passes them to me as we sit on the ground floor of the apartment, next to the washing machine and the water filter that does not work, the vines and monkeys on the other side of the open wall.*

# Ether

The trip up the mountains was scarier than in Rio, where the cab driver had said, "Don't walk that way — ever," and pointed to the left of the entrance to my hotel. From this metropolis, I'd bused to Caxambu, a small town in the state of Minas Gerais, Brazil. Now, I sat with several other spiritual seekers in a small, white, springless van as we tumbled up the rocky red roads to the sacred mountains.

These final four days in the country were to be a period of rest after several weeks in the historical and cultural mecca of Salvador, Bahia. "Finding Oneself: A Call to Renewal" was the name of our retreat. I'd envisioned a few days of recuperation and enlightenment before heading home to Canada.

It soon became clear that I was the only native English speaker in the group. Because of this, I'd been left off the Portuguese language WhatsApp group and was missing the following crucial information. The last three kilometres of the journey up the mountain were to be walked. I wore delicate peach-coloured sandals with a thong-like strap between two toes and three gold medallions of increasing size decorating each foot.

The white van of deliverance deposited us at the bottom of the mountain, turned around, and drove away. I watched sulkily as the others marched onwards with their walking sticks and good shoes, preferring to wait for the truck that would follow with our luggage to take me the rest of the way. I was by myself on the road. Silence. Insects. A slight breeze.

The sound of a motor. A helmeted man with a cinnamon brown face appeared on a motorcycle. He stared as he drove by. When a second man appeared out from the hills on a bicycle, I realized that these seemingly isolated mountains were potentially filled with hikers, cyclists, motorcyclists, and such.

The sky darkened as the sun moved across the horizon. I checked the remaining battery of my cellphone and searched my darkening screen for the flashlight app. I looked morosely at my pretty sandals and swallowed the last of the water in my small plastic bottle. I started to walk.

## Air

My Brazil is like this. Sometimes, things only make sense if one is heat-sunned with the taste of papaya on one's lips, where any conversation or carefully planned excursion can take circuitous routes.

Before arriving at the mountains, I'd spent my last day in Salvador, Bahia, hiding out in a gated suburban community. I'd been desperate to leave the city centre where Carnaval preparations were relentlessly underway. Drumming bands of ten to one hundred people practised in the streets. "They are torturing us!" said one street seller as she handed over my new earrings made of capim, a twisted golden grass. The last straw had been the *pre*-Carnaval parades — delighted locals wearing abadás, matching T-shirts, parading beside blocos — trucks that blared the latest samba-reggae and Carnaval hits. The only way home through the streets of exuberant revellers was to dance with them, up the hill to my neighbourhood of Santo Antônio, separating out from the crowd once I reached the corner of Rua dos Ossos — the street of bones.

In addition to ear fatigue, I'd also needed relief from the high alert of moving through a complex culture. Being a particular shade of brown common among the many afrodescendentes of the state of Bahia, I'd spent weeks negotiating this strange realm of familiar and foreign, a Black gringa. To some I appeared to be Bahiana, just not very bright, as I stood in an awkward silence when my limited Portuguese failed me. I often "passed," which meant that I got the local rate on cachaça, a raw rum sold from barrels. It also meant that I was looked at with wariness when I entered the expensive tourist stores with my cinnamon brownness and inexplicably unlocal sandals. I was often met with endearments and honorifics. An old man reached out to touch me at Samba de Roda, a musical gathering. "Rainha," he said. Queen. And yet, on my return from the suburban beach that last day in Bahia, the guard at the condominium stopped himself mid-sentence from asking, "Which household are you here to work for?"

Now, I was far from such things, walking alone, surrounded by the freshest, quietest air, yet listening for the motorized salvation of a four-wheel drive truck. I checked and re-checked the light on my cellphone, hoping as I rounded each turn to see the rest of my group before me. I had a sense that the long walk up the mountain to the sanctuary was to be part of the journey back to self. "What a dumb idea," I grumbled to myself. Just drive me there, gringo style. When I crested the next hill, I spotted the others far ahead. I ran toward them with relief. They turned as one head, saw me, and waited. The rising darkness that had so concerned me was also that which had caused the resolution of my fear: they'd only stopped to take photos of the setting sun.

## Fire

For the spiritual quest, we were to spend the night in the open air on a rocky mountaintop. Without words or music, and under an invisible coating of Wi-Fi–free air, the stillness was loud. I knew with the absence of distractions that I would be free to hear other things: my own intuition, the voices of nature, those difficult questions that I wanted no part of. I sat in my chosen spot, surrounded by grasses blackened from a recent wildfire and diligent flowers that had willed themselves from the charred earth. I found a walking stick to accompany me, which was burnt at one end, dried branches shooting from the other, like a comet's tail. I had juice, water, a candle, blankets, a raincoat, and a flashlight. I stared out over the neighbouring mountains of rock and shrubs as darkness fell. Then the drums began. I sighed. After a day of water and juice fasting, I did not know if the rhythms reverberating around the mountains were real, played by spirits, or just imaginings brought on by hunger and fatigue.

At some point in the night, I left my collection of damp blankets and manoeuvred through the pitch-dark and scrub grass to the glow of a fire, where the shaman and her assistant kept vigil. "I need to go back down," I said. No, they responded. Push through. Find out what spirit has to tell you. "Spirit says I need to sleep in a bed tonight," I insisted. When a few other shivering seekers joined us at the fire, we were walked back down the mountain trails to our cabins.

# Water

The drums were not spirits after all. A few miles away, under a forest canopy, a group of men were also on a spiritual quest. I suspected that theirs was somewhat more strenuous than our interrupted evening sojourn. Ceremonies, limpezas (ritual baths), pilgrimages, and divinations were everywhere in Brazil. There appeared to be a general thirst for spirit. The traditions of the Indigenous peoples, the religions and rituals of the kidnapped Africans brought to this land between the 1600s and 1800s, have their connections with nature and the elements of earth, wind, fire, and water. They are referenced constantly in Brazilian language, music, and dance. During the previous few weeks in Bahia, I'd often been invited to attend festas at the terreiros — ceremonies at the temples of the Afro-Brazilian religion Candomblé.

It seemed that even the colonialists and enslavers from Europe were looking for salvation. In the city of Salvador, I'd never seen so many churches per square kilometre. Most markedly, the Lavagem do Bonfim, a six-kilometre pilgrimage from the Church of Conceição da Praia through the streets, was the height of syncretism of these spiritual solitudes. The route is followed each year by the Filhos de Gandhy, a famous men's group who combine the teachings of Gandhi with African traditions, and hundreds of other spiritual and musical groups. Thousands of pilgrims and tourists join in, all dressed in white. Upon arrival at the end point, the Church of Nosso Senhor do Bonfim, one can pay for the blessings of a Candomblé priest, push through the crowds of food vendors and capoeira practitioners, and tie a fita or coloured ribbon bearing the name of an Afro-Brazilian Orixá onto the Catholic church's wrought iron gates.

We all want to be cleansed of sorrow, pain, bad decisions. I'd just never seen this desire repeated overtly in so many forms. The ritual bath in the mountains of Minas Gerais, under a waterfall, felt a lot like the limpeza in the terreiro where I'd crouched naked in a small dark concrete shower room and been splashed with a minty-smelling concoction of herbs. Even on the island haven off the coast of Salvador, holidayers cover themselves in yellow clay from the cliffs of Gamboa do Morro and then dash into the sea to become clean again.

## Earth

After four days, it was time to head home. Difficult questions had arisen and, with the counsel of the shaman, had dissipated or been resolved and I felt sufficiently enlightened. The way back down the hills ended much as it had begun. Walking. The white van that was to return us to Caxambu was not at the arranged meeting place that morning. The others, all Brazilian, just shrugged. A passing cyclist stopped and asked, "Are you waiting for a van?" Yes. "There is one waiting down the hill." Why is it waiting there, and not waiting where it dropped us off a few days ago? Because we are in Brazil and it's just like that. I sighed, shook my head. I had a bus to catch, to get me to São Paulo and my flight back to Canada. We walked back down the cursed road. "I hate Brazil," I said under my breath in a flash of frustration. Instantly, one of my fellow seekers tripped on the slippery red rocks, and her walking stick flipped upwards and smacked me in the shin. She smiled, shrugged. "Desculpa." Sorry.

Here, instant karma and other gifts arise as a matter of course. Food is sun-kissed. Snacks are ground provisions and an egg, or tapioca melted into a flat crêpe and filled with cheese and guava jam. When people don't have much material to offer, they hold each other, both friends and strangers, in greeting, with a smile or an endearment. We don't do that easily where I come from. I'd been held by nature as well, the air, the muddy red earth and the soft fire of a sunset that stopped my fellow travellers, so that I could find them.

I catch my bus to São Paulo and my plane home.

On a Saturday afternoon in Toronto, music spills out of the curtained doorway of a small bar onto the sidewalk of Davenport Road. Inside, a drummer pounds on a giant surdo with a padded mallet. He is joined by other musicians playing cavaquinho, violão, and pandeiro. This is Roda de Samba, a gathering of Brazilian music aficionados that takes place every few weeks. The community jumps and spins and sings along. It feels like a cleansing, a limpeza of sound. I sit still for a second on the wooden bench that runs along a red brick wall and tell an acquaintance of my time in the sacred mountains of Minas Gerais. "I've been there many times," he says. "That mountaintop is usually covered in clouds and fog. Did you have any clear days?" Yes, the mountains stretched endlessly before us. We had four days of spectacular clarity. He stares at me, eyes wide.

"That never happens."

# The Mathematics of Rage

Sitting at Northwood on Bloor Street West over a mocktail and a beer, Gillian asks, "Did you notice suddenly becoming invisible to men at around age forty?"

Me: "Nope."

"Yeah, but you are beautiful."

"So are you."

"But I noted it and it was sudden." Gillian is smart, gorgeous, accomplished, brilliant, white, a writer, and one of my mentors during my MFA.

Good for her, I thought, as mostly, I found myself far too visible. Still. A constant imposition or a weight lay upon me. Except, that is, when I wanted medical or legal care or psychological or academic care for me or my child — then I became eminently less visible, categorically unseen, a giant perplexity for someone who looked at me blankly, or with sexually laced assumptions or suspicion.

This is not unlike my trip to a walk-in medical clinic for extreme rib pain that had me hobbled. After an hour wait, I was sent to an examining room. The doctor entered. I sat twisted in pain and pointed at my aching chest. His face turned to scorn, the absence of concern. "Get out," he said. "Just, just go," he said, waving me and my pain away.

It happens to women of all races and ages, this shifting state of value and visibility. Gillian noted herself as suddenly unseen at a certain age. My Blackness, however, ensures that eyes remain on me. This disappears, however, when I am due for a promotion or am in need of care. Then, I am fucking invisible.

I did not respond in real time at the clinic. My thoughts were blunted by pain, shock, and confusion. This medical assault surprised and shocked me, and yet it did not surprise me at all. The doctor assumed I was there for opiates. He was an Asian man, not white as some might assume. Majority culture tropes and assumptions can be absorbed by anyone, including ourselves. The receptionist who had watched me squirming in pain during my hour-long wait to be seen, looked up startled as I left approximately one minute after the doctor entered my examining room.

The doctor got paid by our state for that visit. For my pain-infused walk to and presence in the walk-in clinic, I got nothing. The next day, after another pain-filled night, I took more time off from my own job and visited a naturopath who was also a chiropractor. I paid for this visit myself. Upon a physical examination that took approximately two minutes, he determined I had a dislocated rib. "What have you done to yourself?" he asked. "This is a body response. Have you been under extreme stress?"

"You have no idea," I responded.

•

"An elegant theorem is just like a woman," my university calculus professor would say as he waved his hands around, outlining the curves of breasts and hips. He did a powerful Performance of Calculus, prancing back and forth across the auditorium where we sat before him in ascending rows. He scribbled streams of numbers, letters, and symbols on the blackboard. He showed us magical mathematical formulas that could be used to solve complex problems.

He'd brush back a thick lock of grey-black hair from his forehead for emphasis of key concepts. Sometimes he would leave us with a marvel of an equation to take home and appreciate its majesty on our own time. I loved calculus even though I did not calculate well. I loved its complexity and digging deep into possibility. The nebulous space of the theoretical. I propose queries and theorems to myself when other language does not quite fit experience.

If you are tossed out of a medical clinic when requesting care, leaving with physical pain intact, are you a person or a phantasm of the doctor's mind? If an invention, how do you solve the unseeing imposition on your very self? Do you speak, rail against it, explain that you are real? Is it worth the expulsion of energy to explain that a woman with dreads might not be trying to score drugs?

Can I express anger about this? If not, where does the anger go? Does it sit in my flesh, in the muscles of my back, shoulders, or gut? Does it inhabit my blood cells and twist my ribs into further harm? The body speaks its own language. It howls at inequity. It rages upon itself, expressing emotional pain, social dysfunction, with such wounds. If I need relief from such pain, am I simultaneously required to teach that I am human and not the invention living within in the eyes of my interlocutor?

At work, I once took a course where you were asked to determine what currency you find valuable — that is, what do you find valuable, in terms of an exchange for work? What is an energetic exchange that is acceptable to you? The course proposed money, status, or learning as options. I chose learning, as I did not have access to other stuff like, oh, increased salary or promotion. For years, the currency of my energy was decreased to one value. I am far too familiar with being randomly unseen. What is an appropriate response to this?

Is it better to raise my voice in frustration? Or is it better to be silent, to leave and go get help somewhere safe without additional assault to the being? How do we get from here to there with the least amount of harm to our very selves? Why must we relentlessly calculate safety, spending our energetic currency in an environment that hates us? All of us Black women make these rapid, complex, chess-like calculations on the arithmetic of the heart.

Don't get mad back. Do not get angry at imposition. Smile. Bend your head slightly. Accept. Take it in. Yes, that's better. Keeps you safe. Smile. And certainly, do not feel grief for your small girl-self who does not understand that she is held in the fist of a wilful and violent absence.

In her essay "Power Walking," Scottish and Sierra Leonean writer Aminatta Forna points out that these and other impositions, these decisions to oversee/not see, are learned behaviours. She describes noting a young white man staring at her, a Black woman twice his age. He smirks when he notes her noting him. Forna then has a moment of insight. He is practising. He is enacting a version of his culture, what it tells him to do, where power lies and over whom and how to enact it. He has created a power play with a stranger who is not part of the duel.

Forna writes:

> Nobody tells young girls that men own the power
> of the gaze. My mother never told me that men
> may look at me but I may not look back. That
> if we do our look can be taken as an invitation.
> Men teach us that. Over the years we train our

gaze to skim men's faces, resting for only a split second shifting fractionally sideways if our eyes happen to meet. The man on the other hand, if he so wishes, will look at your face, your breasts, your legs, your ass....

The gaze is power. Men own the power of the gaze. White people do, too.... They stare because they can, by the gift of the power vested in them by their membership in the ethnic majority....

When a man stares at a woman in public her sensitivities are, at the very least, immaterial to him. He owns the power of the gaze and he will, if he cares to, exercise it. The real mindfuck is that enfolded into the action is its defence. The woman who complains may well find herself being told, she should be flattered, that she is lucky men find her attractive.[1]

*Physical body + gaze = increased value? If perpetually mis-seen, am I beautiful, a criminal, or a walking ghost?*

•

My partner and I have been together for two years. He is still not used to it. In the beginning, he'd asked, what is going on? Do you always get this much attention? Does this always happen to you? And then finally, how do you manage?

Welcome to my world of constant visibility, I said. Sit tight. We are going to walk from here to there — a distance of about six blocks. Can you cope? I ask. He walks with me and feels stares, my body perused despite his presence or perhaps because of it as well, by whomever.

*Ordinary physique + female + Blackness = extraordinary gaze, imposition, attention, social permission to gawk. Often by men — sometimes by women.*

One night, I'd tried to sleep after a night of bad music in a shit venue and felt a deep weight on my chest that would not let me breathe without pain. Earlier in the evening, a lone white woman had circled me and my partner, flicking long gazes at him, checking me to see if I'd noticed. My partner became increasingly furious and disgusted, watching her watch us, disbelieving this complex at play.

We, a Black woman and white man, are a social trigger. I know this. I am familiar with little pieces of crazy that can drop out of nowhere on a night out. Often my response has been a help-less attempt to ignore such attentions, while monitoring my own emotional safety. My partner asks, "Who is that? And why is she checking us and sniffing our asses?" I explain the above. However, when someone yells at me, "I hate mixed couples," then threatens, "You better get out of here 'sis,'" what is an appropriate response?

•

I am privileged in many ways. I am educated in western institutions and sit solidly in the lower-middle class income level. Regardless, the constant social pressures — medical, legal, academic, work-place — still add up.

Idil Abdillahi, in her book *Black Women Under State: Surveillance, Poverty, & the Violence of Social Assistance*, notes that despite being a professor or a grad student, a certain "unbelievability" has been built up around our very existence. "I understood that there truly has never been a time when we have been afforded that believability. Even as a child, there is no particular moment I can reflectively mark where this inherent regard — believability, deservingness, and trust-edness — was afforded by the culture around me."[2]

Multiple articles and studies note that incidences of hypertension and heart disease among Black women are elevated when compared to other demographics, and that we are often disbelieved and undertreated when we experience pain.

So when later that same night, I ended up in Emergency with general heart pain, I was frightened. First of all, I realized the cumulative effect of repeated experiences and that an additional gram of misogynoir could send me into physical distress. My mind wandered back to the experience in the walk-in clinic. I wondered if my pain would be taken seriously; if they, the triage nurse, knew I was part of a demographic at high risk for hypertension and stroke. I wondered if I would be treated differently if I looked more like, or exactly like my partner, a tall white man. Would I have been whisked away to a special room and given a battery of tests? I knew that a heart attack manifests differently in women, with strange arm pains and wandering discomforts. The almost immediate EKG sticker, placed on my file, assuaged my concerns somewhat. We were sent down a long hallway to another waiting area already full of people. The EKG was done relatively quickly. The nurse took a sample of my blood for testing.

During the hours-long wait for lab results, we watched infants seen immediately, their tiny bodies needing instant care. I knew this from having brought my own baby, limp in my arms, and being told to sit and wait. I'm from a medical family. I knew what the hospital staff needed to hear. I also knew that a distressed and loud Black woman would be an embarrassment for them. "Five-month-old baby, vomiting bile, completely dehydrated, and fading fast. Needs to be seen now!" I yelled. We were hurried through double doors into the hidden recesses of care. She did not die.

Now, as we sat for four hours waiting to be seen, I felt the pain in my chest shifting and subsiding for moments at a time. Since I was not in acute distress, I gathered that perhaps the EKG showed nothing overtly wrong. Was it just some kind of panic attack or something more subversive?

We watched the workings of the ER waiting room, which involved a circle of nurses and clerks enclosed behind plastic barriers. One doctor would occasionally race past us, visit a few patients, and then disappear for an hour to another section of the hospital. He'd then race back for another stint in our section. I wondered if there was only one doctor on call, covering two rooms.

Eventually, I was placed on a bed, panels separating me from others on both sides. The doctor stopped in front of me, holding a chart. He listened to my concerns about the pain, which had by now mostly subsided. He perused my chart. Then he said, "In ER we are really good at the big bad stuff. We are less good at the subtleties. Blood work is good. EKG is good. There is no big bad stuff."

Okay, I said. Thank you. I did wonder, however, if the blood work done to determine the presence of proteins indicated by a heart attack also included a screening for drugs in my system.

It's complex and exhausting work, this incorporation of shifting variables — a relentless assessment of scenarios to determine the level of safety, the recalibration of self to calm, and perhaps a moment of equanimity — but it is just one of the multiple layers of psychic work we do.

Dr. Jennifer Mullan is also known as the Rage Doctor. She sees rage as an appropriate response to constant systemic harm and the energetic work required to relentlessly counter, avoid, or recover from it. She also suggests that rage is deeply connected to unresolved grief. Generations of it. Impositions and violence inflicted on generations sit with the body/mind. Ancestral trauma can come to sit in the genes, as described in relatively new scientific developments of epigenetics and social genomics. It is carried in the body and passed on. It is then reinforced when systems that caused them remain intact.

The perpetual requirement to assess surroundings, negotiate, and self-regulate for the payoff of being left in peace is a weight. Nature shows us that growth can be like fractals, circling and expanding. If it is good, it's good. If it is a weight that is onerous, it grows exponentially until the heart bleeds and you fall down.

My partner sat quietly at my side through the emergency department experience. This was a very small maze. Nothing really. Not in the big scheme of life. I need an intervention, however, as I will not do this again. I will listen to my heart before it screams at me. I will make change. I will dissolve, if I can, that which sits internally, waiting to devour me.

·

Years ago, I'd taken the ferry to Toronto Island, to drift along the boardwalks in a semi-natural environment. This oasis was a contrast to my rooms in a soon-to-be-condemned building at Sherbourne and Bloor, full of actors and musicians living cheap. I happened upon a celebration, a powwow. I sat in a circle, next to a woman in a long colourful skirt, who would soon become a friend. We guided each other for a time. Bobbi was an Indigenous woman who pulled me into women's circles at the Native Canadian Centre on Spadina Avenue and in the homes of Elders. I attended these sacred healing times for a few years.

At times some Elders preferred Indigenous women only.

"You need to come. You're Carib. You can come," she'd insist.

I don't identify as an Indigenous person, and doing so would be disingenuous, I told her. I can respect the Elders' preferences.

I get it. I'm good with that. Sometimes, Black women also want a circle for themselves, for privacy, to heal specific pains, to share specific experiences, insights, and wisdoms. "I'll see you another time," I told Bobbi. I can wait for an Elder who is good with me, a Black woman participating and learning. I'd seen impositions enacted on my own communities as the dominant cultural group or gender took up aural, emotional, and psychic space, pulling focus in someone else's home, centralizing selves at an event, a circle, a prayer, a dance.

We, Bobbi and I, had had vastly different experiences, with parallels in the existence and impact of generational trauma. I will not speak for her. I can only hold this pain, which reverberates and echoes with some of my own. I still carry a violent loss of peoples kidnapped on the African continent and forced to the Americas in my bones. I can acknowledge the history, experience, and loss of others. Later economic migrants, who travel far in order to live, have their cultures currently pillaged by the same entities that pillaged ours.

The young Mexican guy who cleans my building keeps his head down, avoids all eye contact. If you don't see, you might remain unseen, invisible, out of harm's way. One day he looked up, briefly skimmed my face. "Hi," I said. One day he might say hello back.

•

In the 1960s, Dr Pepper was reimagined as a hot drink to be served with lemon as an aperitif at dinner parties. It has fruit in it, the voice-over claimed. It was a fantastical, imaginary scenario dreamed up by ad men in a room and then filmed with attractive people sipping the heated pop, ladled into glasses from a large glass bowl. The ad showed how to slice the garnish of lemon as well. Pop reinvented as the drink of would-be aristocrats at a cocktail party. The white people were pretty. The gaze of the camera returned to the blond woman, with straight hair flipped up at the ends, just past shoulder length, the style sewn onto the rubbery heads of all of my Barbie dolls.

I wondered why this pissed me off when I wandered across it on YouTube, this conglomeration of shit information, images, and sugar. Because this image, this profile is still around. Because linked to my unseen, mis-seen, over-seen self, this ideal and this way of seeing persists. Which means, Gillian has slipped out of a kind of attention with age and I am here, certain attentions intact.

More than thirty years later, there are now many more options of media to view. I think there always has been something, it was just inaccessible. With new technologies streaming at us, a few days after watching the Dr Pepper ad, the following rolled into my algorithmic sphere — a video by Sampa The Great, "Never Forget," with Chef 187, Tio Nason, and Mwanjé. I think it's the best video on the internet. No, really. Its images, fabric, bodies, words, and sounds are like rich oily paintings in motion. Complex histories inhabit and are transmitted with each frame.

"Future ancient," she says, and I feel the juxtaposition of these words as sweet and profound, holding worlds and possibility.

Sampa The Great's song is a reclamation. The process of reclaiming is a response, an action that acknowledges something was taken. The song exudes rage.

The video goes beyond mere reaction to deep knowledge, showing self to self. Maybe this is what artist and writer Marva Jackson Lord means when she says rage can be "a fuel for constructive transformation." Maybe this is also what meditation teacher, social activist, and author Ruth King leans toward in her book *Healing Rage: Women Making Inner Peace Possible*, a throughway that she points to, smiling.

What could my transformation look like? Perhaps writing out the unnamed is my beginning. My ins and outs with the hospital system have been few. Even as I experienced dismissal when going to a walk-in clinic, I have been lucky.

I will, however, call these experiences in and name them. If I name them, I bless the unacknowledged, the stuff that slips by unaccounted for. If too much remains unnoted, we live in a vacuum, an unbearable place. Instead, I am learning a language that can hold our external and cellular worlds and our invisible psychic spaces. I will begin here, looking for an equation to hold our worth.

# Passage

t begins with a dream. Not mine. In 1865, August Kekulé, a German chemist, was confounded by a puzzle of molecular structure: How could six atoms of carbon and six atoms of hydrogen, each with a limited number of bonding sites, come together to form the stable compound benzene?

This would have been the year before the British grabbed Ghana from the Portuguese; the year France was ruled by Napoleon III, who had followed in his uncle's brutal foreign policy shoes; the year the British government passed the Indian Forest Act, staking claim over the forests of India. It is also possibly the year that the Taino of the Caribbean islands were declared extinct. Their disappearance is imaginary yet convenient, supporting the idea of empty lands waiting for the taking — an illusion of stability.

One hundred and thirty years later, I'd just graduated with a degree in biology. I'd returned to the laboratory to pick up a knap-sack my lab instructor had left for me in one of the cupboards. As I ran my hand along the Formica top of my spot in the lab, I recalled days and evenings spent on the mandatory first-year biology fruit fly experiment. We'd bred the insects in jars, and every few days we'd etherize a batch of flies. We'd then pull apart the mounds of dead bodies with tweezers and place them under a Nikon microscope to see whether they had blue, red, or green eyes. The goal of this exercise was to teach us the basics of genetics. It was an inexact methodology. Sometimes eye colour was hard to discern, as it depended on the light coming through the windows, the quality of the food in our stomachs from the university cafeteria, or how drunk we were on etheric fumes. Sometimes the eye colour appeared as a purplish mix of blue and red. We could assign it to one category or the other. Sometimes we would write "mixed."

I was making my way through the laboratory, opening and closing the cupboard doors as I searched for my knapsack, when a man came in.

"What are you doing here?"

"I'm looking for something left for me by my lab instructor."

My lab. My university. My stuff. Scowling, he watched me. Livid. Suspicious. Of course, no bag had been left for me. My lab instructor had either forgotten or hadn't bothered to place it in our agreed-upon spot. I left the building under the hostile gaze of this white man, his perception of me as an intruder intruding upon me.

I'd enjoyed some of my studies in science during my years at Queen's University. In Ecology 101, we learned about scientific method by chasing squirrels around the university grounds, counting the number of "hops" versus "runs." In Fungus 100, I was entranced by the organisms under a microscope. I saw them as minute and intricate landscapes of rolling fields and forests. I had a much more complex relationship with organic chemistry, however. Even as I found it impossible to work out the chemical formulas of most compounds, I loved it best, the way you love a recalcitrant child, inexplicable yet compelling, with all your heart. I knew within it was some mystery of invisible bonds I was seeking to touch.

•

The lowly milk snake is under ecological pressure. Why? Partially, because we, humans, keep running over them, along with turtles and other wildlife, with our cars. Due to wisdom gleaned in first-year ecology, I knew that the solution might have been something simple. Perhaps while creatures are trying to cross the asphalt roads slapped down onto their habitat, to move from one part of their world to another, to mate or to find food, we could just not run over them. Maybe snakes stop to sun themselves on a spot of warm asphalt occasionally, as even reptiles get tired of always being cold-blooded.

The solution developed by scientists to stop snakes and other organisms from being run over by cars was to dig a passageway under the road, a culvert as it were, to provide them with safe passage. Connecting one bit of habitat to another is termed connectivity. This solution is a lackadaisical and expensive apology that does not require that we change our system. We want cars and convenience. We live here now. We are, however, ill at ease with ourselves. We fret over the well-being of wildlife even as we continue to build roads through their habitats. We pay scientists to do research on how to save them. Maybe *we* need to lie in the sun for a bit, to not be so damn cold-blooded.

•

In the 1800s, while Kekulé was searching for the structure of this substance made of six carbon and six hydrogen atoms, swaths of Indigenous people were disappeared, populations of buffalo made almost extinct, and enslaved Black people brought up from the United States of America with United Empire Loyalist owners and set to clearing the lands around the Rouge Valley. No, wait, the lands were taken and bequeathed to many white people, among them the Pennsylvania Dutch Mennonites, who soon became some of the biggest landowners in the region. The rich soil of these gentle hills soon made them rich overseers of agriculture. I have often wondered where all the others who were present on these lands at that time have gone. Who else is in the carefully tended cemeteries in the Rouge? Let's dig a little more deeply, shall we?

All things are connected, even if we don't want them to be. The thing about people of African descent in the Americas is that we can easily glean when there are a Black grandmother's genes in those hips or a flounce of hair, when there is an unexpected flourish of brownness with a too-long moment in the sun. We know that the world is like this: a dandelion pierces through a crack in the asphalt of a country road; the unseen is revealed in the inexplicably full lips of the third brother in the sib-line of the white founding farming families.

Kekulé solved his puzzle. In a daydream, the image of a snake eating its own tail arose. This spherical form revealed how the molecules of carbon could bond together to form benzene.

"I love benzene!" Margaret, a fellow writer who also has science degrees trailing in her wake, said to me. Finally, someone who understood the joy in the perfection of its neat, understandable formula. It was clear, finite; atoms held neatly together by invisible bonds, a kind of poetry in its toxic perfection. In this understanding of an iota of organic chemistry, I felt clever. It was also the perfect symmetry of a closed system. A closed system is also a kind of death. The naturally found chemical benzene can kill you.

•

A system can be operationally closed, like a sphere or social system that communicates only with itself. According to writer and scholar Sara Ahmed, if I walk by a group of people all speaking Russian and I do not understand, I cannot enter that communication system. It is operationally closed to me. Nothing new comes in. Shut like a mind. Even as Ahmed refers to herself as a feminist killjoy, I find that her work makes me joyful. She says that a closed system can be opened up. We don't have to speak the same language to feel an invisible bond start to grow as we gaze at each other. Expectation extends beyond the limits of language.

·

It is 2015. A long driveway past a curated garden on one side and a tiny patch of trees and bush on the other leads to a farmhouse that has been converted into an office. This is where I worked in a job vaguely connected to my science degree. One morning, we arrived at work to find a deer and its fawn standing close to the barn. Once they saw us, the animals retreated into the trees. They'd peek out from the foliage throughout the day, curious, perhaps hungry. We could see them from the windows of our desks in the farmhouse.

A decision was made by ecological and urban wildlife experts that we were to stand down and let nature take its course. I heard someone refer to the patch of trees at the corner of Kingston and Markham Road as a habitat. Two weeks later, the fawn appeared alone on the driveway. Perhaps the mother had left in the night, finding her way back home, the fawn unable or, like a recalcitrant child, unwilling to follow. Again, the wildlife and ecological experts said, leave it alone: let nature in the city take its course. What might be natural in this scenario? The pavements, spots of park that might or might not lead to a patch of forest? It seemed a cruel analysis.

Bits of forests of various sizes are woven into the Rouge Valley, which is a strange mix of apartment buildings, farms, single-family homes, highways, public parks, trails, and, yes, forests. This patchwork of living environments for humans and wildlife has been gathered together under one name, the Rouge National Urban Park. I checked maps for interlocking trails of green that crossed the park, joining patches of trees. I looked for how the deer might have made it to the office grounds and how they might make it back through the neural network of concrete streets and patches of green, trails, highways, and bridges to a larger forest.

Creating connectivity between systems requires mechanisms of various kinds. A culvert with appropriate fencing will lead wildlife like snakes or even deer under a highway to safe ground on the other side. A well-made bridge can do that as well. It, too, can join micro-habitats allowing passage, like an invisible highway, an underground railroad, linkages opened up by hope and expectation of a freer life.

The mother deer might have found her way back to a larger wood. Maybe she'd become easy pickings for a suburban hunter. There had been an issue with a crossbow down the street last summer. With its mother gone, the fawn settled on a patch of lawn between the farmhouse and a parking lot. It would stand up alert each time someone walked by. Eventually, due to fatigue, loneliness, and hunger, it took to lying down all day in the sun. It became thin.

I once met a shaman. Malidoma Somé told me that he is a bridge. He links two points, Burkina Faso and the West. He then told me, "You, too, are a bridge, only it is much more complex." He was referring to the many continents and heritages held within my being. Perhaps, like the trails, culverts, bridges, I carry invisible songlines, recipes, and histories from one place to another. Sometimes a wildlife corridor is an idea, a breath between cultures.

The fawn was eventually taken in by a wildlife organization, perhaps via the mechanism of a small van.

•

In my last year of university, I had a job in the lab cleaning up radioactive isotopes left by sloppy fourth-year students. One of a series of shit jobs that I undertook during my life. There was always shit work on offer.

I circled my way out and beyond it, slithering under, through asphalt, building a different kind of bridge over imposed limitations slapped onto my brown skin. Opening up a system. Circling is my way through the seemingly untenable life of being a writer. In this constant motion, I find the deepest stability, as here I am most myself.

In this state, the body will not stay still. My mind is busy even when sleep-like. I am told that I mumble all night long, tying up leads, connecting spiritual habitats. Sometimes I dream of the shining compound eyes of a mound of dead fruit flies. Sometimes I dream that I am a five-pointed bridge, a star of neural networks. Sometimes I dream that a snake slithers into the darkness of a culvert and travels safely to the other side of the road.

***Remedy*** — *I only aspire to be a polyglot, dropping in worlds from other languages into my speech to hold what I really mean. Perhaps that is why I enjoy the polyglots and the non-binaries and the mixed folk, artists, and healers who will not stay in one psychic space, who jump tracks, layers, and worlds with ease. A gesture can be a healing. Some have always known art is medicine.*

# Music Notes

Once a week my guitar teacher would walk up the slight hill to the small colonial-style house on Hermitage Road, Belmont, Trinidad. Mr. Sonny Denner was tall, sharply dressed in a brown suit and tie. As he uncased his guitar, I would set up two hard-backed chairs in a corner of the living room. In our home, music was sacrosanct. My brothers and parents tiptoed over the wooden floors, so as not to disturb my lessons, which often wandered into the two-and-a-half-hour range.

My guitar was an obzokie creature with an inexplicably thick neck that made it hard for me to play. To reach the frets on the front, my eight-year-old hands would have to stretch — thumb at back, fingers on the front. The steel strings were taut and deep purple grooves would develop on my fingertips as the lessons progressed. For reasons known only to him, the first song he taught me was from a 1954 American musical, *The Pajama Game*. "Hernando's Hideaway," a tune covered by everyone from Ella Fitzgerald to Doris Day, was a combination of genres — Euro classical, hints of jazz and Spanish music. This may have set the tone for what I was open to hearing and playing for years to come. He wrote out the melody on a sheet of staff paper and placed it on the music stand in front of us. I was a slow reader of notes, my fingertips were always sore, and the lessons would not end. My little girl-self felt, however, that some core of what he was teaching me was very important and so, I found ways to continue. To give my fingertips some respite and to avoid reading, I would ask him to play "Hernando's Hideaway" a few more times. I would watch his hands with deep attention and memorize the shapes his fingers made. I would then play back a mirror image of what I'd seen, while looking meaningfully at the carefully written sheet music.

When my father brought home a new guitar, I was ecstatic. Mr. Jules Louis, who crafted guitars and cuatros for calypso and parang in his workshop on Gloster Lodge Road, had made my new instrument. It was a child-sized guitar with nylon strings. My fingertips no longer turned purple during long lessons. My reading habits, however, were set. I continued to scan a manuscript in a general fashion, noting keys, codas, and tempos. I'd combine this with memorizing my teacher's hand positions. I had long slim fingers that landed precisely on the appropriate frets at the appropriate times.

We moved to a new neighbourhood of Petit Valley a year or two later. Even though Mr. Denner did not follow, he remained a critical influence. Music sat soundly in my worlds now in a place beyond listening, an invisible thread, that I clung to over the multiple moves that would follow.

In my new bedroom, I sat low on my chair, left foot on the six-inch metal footstool, nylon-stringed guitar cradled between my thighs. Before me was a music stand that held a thin white book. Due to her persistent request, I'd agreed to play something for a cousin. Perhaps she had expected something more familiar, some kaiso, like the Mighty Sparrow's "Drunk & Disorderly" or Lord Kitchener's "Rain-O-Rama" or Shadow's "Bass Man" — all of which I would strum along to. Instead, I played a gavotte by J.S. Bach. She twisted up her face, saying, "What is that?" I watched her turn away, laughing. I hung my head in disappointment and humiliation. I quietly got up and closed the door to my room, and with that gesture, shut out the idea of audience.

My bedroom shared a wall with the grey concrete sink in the backyard of shaddock and banana trees. Outside, as she did every Wednesday, Gwendolyn the washerwoman squeezed and scrubbed the week's clothes on a grey aluminum washboard. Dawn, our sway-backed Alsatian, panted close by in a spot of shade. An Indian man swung his cutlass attached at right angles to a thick wooden stick in circles over his head. Slashing around the shaddock, coconut, and banana trees, he expertly willed the patchy grass of the front yard to exactly 1.5 inches above the ground. I played on inside my room, a safe distance away from the judgment of others, unseen, for the next decade or so, études and gavottes wafting safely around my head.

• 

We moved to Labrador a few years later. I was without a music teacher for the first time. I did have other things to learn here, though. And quickly.

"If you try to walk over there from here, you could get lost and die," my new friend Marylyn said. She pointed to the small field separating my house from Goose High School. During a "whiteout," the snowfall would be so thick that the ground and sky would become one blanket of white. Marylyn cautioned me that every winter someone would wander disoriented for hours, a few feet from their destination.

At Goose High, situated on the Goose Bay military base, cultural orientation was provided by my grade nine classmates. When I stood up as the teacher entered the room, as was the custom in Trinidad's British school system, Eugene pulled me back into my seat. I was two years ahead of my peers academically and Marylyn coached me to keep that quiet. Sherry Ann introduced me to bowling and "fish 'n' brewis." She showed me how the concoction of stale bread, oil, and bits of salted cod were assembled. She presented it to me with pride. I smiled and inwardly balked. I thought, poor people do the same thing everywhere — make do — and then their inventions of survival become a national speciality — fish 'n' brewis in Canada, souse — pickled pig feet and snout in Trinidad and variations of fried white flour both there and here·— baked bake, fried bake, bannock.

She also asked me a strange question. "What is it like to be Black?" Coming from Trinidad's multicultural society, the tragic look on her face was perplexing to me.

I learned quickly that race would be pinned to my forehead like a badge; obscenities could be hurled at me by a white man from a car as I walked home from school in one city, or past a movie lineup in another; that people might behave strangely with various manifestations of overt and often covert aggressions.

My musical education continued in a new fashion as my world of classical guitar, calypso, jazz, and Cuban music fused with the new sounds of K-tel records. These LPs were compilations of random pop songs by the likes of Hall & Oates and Al Stewart. I breathed in these new sounds. I also bought my first rock opera LP, the raging tales on *Alice Cooper Goes to Hell*. Diana Ross's "Theme from Mahogany" was big that year, too, and the Goose High School's non-dancer gym teacher took it upon herself to choreograph a routine to it.

"It's simple and stupid," I complained to my mother. "And she put me in the front."

My mother laughed. "You can't blame her," she said. "You're the only piece of mahogany she has." I liked Diana Ross and I liked dancing, and so, grudgingly, for four minutes, I became the dancing bit of Blackness in school of the white kids of military personnel and three Innu kids from Happy Valley.

•

My father, a Canadian military officer, was next posted to North Bay. The family followed. Here, Canadian music icons Rush and April Wine were introduced to my aural landscape. I now had another guitar teacher. Steve Ranny was a bespectacled young white man with curly black hair and a sweet smile. He accommodated my requests to play through the songs repeatedly, as I secretly memorized his finger movements.

Years later, I toyed with my parents' dream that perhaps one of their three kids might take up their medical professions by studying science at university. I continued to take private guitar lessons on the side. My teacher, Eli, also bespectacled, smelled faintly of cigars. With each new teacher I was gathering gestures and ways of listening, a musical lineage of sorts that grounded me in my shifting worlds. At times I could glimpse through their eyes and ears who I might become.

"You should audition for the music faculty," Eli announced one day. He turned briefly to smile at his sleepy wife who was always just emerging from the bedroom, rubbing her eyes and stretching. "You'd get in," he stated. I froze at the suggestion. Switch from science to music? I knew that pursuing a degree in music would be a zero-sum game with my professional Caribbean family. Yes, music was revered; however, my dad had often told me that to succeed in this world, I — the Black person — would have to work ten times as hard as everyone else —meaning white people. I knew that he did not mean practise ten times more scales on the classical guitar. Making a living was also revered by my family, and this music business was not a great money-making prospect. My family had always surmised that my extended childhood lessons were possibly because Mr. Denner was waiting for my mother to finish cooking dinner and invite him to join us for what was perhaps the only meal of his day.

By this time, I had years ago retired the Jules Louis guitar, the steel-stringed purple-fingertip maker, as well as a more utilitarian Yamaha. I was exclusively playing a work of art. I'd gone to the studio of luthier Oskar Graf to choose the wood for my guitar's spruce top and rosewood sides. It had an elegant cutaway and, of course, the requisite nylon strings.

My classical guitar duet partner, Monica, was an English literature major from Berlin. We understood each other completely. We carefully filed the nails of our right hands with ascending gauges of sandpaper from the hardware store while discussing right-hand technique. We played our François Couperin duet repeatedly with great feel and dynamics in each other's dormitory rooms. We entertained the idea of performance, as one would glance sideways at a strange phenomenon that was interesting but could not fully hold our interest. She understood that an audition involved performing beyond the comfort of my room. She fully supported my reticence. I did not do it.

•

My mother noted my passion for classical guitar and, in an attempt to keep me focused on a more reasonable vocation, would offer the following:

"You can be a doctor, and play your music for your patients in the waiting room," she told me. I imagined a sea of patients in my waiting room, as I had seen in my parents' medical office. I imagined me in a secret room with a music stand and footstool, carefully playing without audience, while still being well heard. She said that I could record my music and pipe the calming tunes into the waiting room. Music as another type of care.

The problem with that vision was that I liked the science part of pre-med courses, but in a more poetic and mystical kind of way. I liked the aesthetics of large glossy black-and-white photographs of bacteria taken with an electron microscope and kept one pasted to the wall of my university dormitory room. Despite achieving good marks in the appropriate classes, studying medicine was far from my sphere of interest. My favourite science course had been the World of Fungi, where I delighted in the miniature landscapes, rises, and treelike protrusions. I imagined minuscule people and creatures moving through a magical world of lichen, which appeared as miniature ferns and pines under our desktop Nikons. I dreamed of walking through their delicate multicoloured landscapes. My lab partner dressed in long grey blanket capes and was not destined to be a scientist either. She talked about her plans to return to her community to marry a chief named Dale. I talked of drawing, music, poetry. Both of us were dreamy, living beyond the walls of the biology building. My lab partner got out first, returning to her reserve. I knew that this was not for me either, but it took me another year to leave. I completed my degree, knowing full well that, despite my love of microscopic fungal landscapes, the poetry of calculus, and the elegant formulae of organic chemistry, doctor who plays guitar on the side was not going to work out.

•

Sometime after university and a circuitous route to avoid studying medicine that involved a diploma in fashion design, I found a job at a clothing design studio in Toronto. There were other passions at work within me, however. Along with playing classical guitar in the spare moments of my twenty-something-year-old life, I was exploring other modes of expression and also writing poetry. In my desire to locate my freest self, I ended up, oddly enough, finding a space of healing within a world where performance was a requirement for participation. In the basement of a church at Huron and Bloor, a few subway stops away from the design studio, Ed and Ray set up chairs, tables, and a tiny sound system with two microphones to host Fat Albert's — the city's longest-running open stage. Anyone could arrive early Wednesday evening, trudge down a flight of stairs to the cave-like space, and get a number that would determine the order of performers for the night. Each person had a few minutes to perform anything for the length of about two songs. I would nervously read my poems out loud, paper shaking in my hands. Surrounded by people with guitars singing folk songs and, knowing that I could play guitar, too, I brought the Oskar Graf to the room one night. The night of my inaugural guitar-playing performance, I sat on stage, guitar between my legs, left foot on the carefully placed footstool, and played "Canzonetta" by Felix Mendelssohn. My hands shook and I could barely hold them in place on the fretboard.

I developed a routine. Each Wednesday afternoon, before making my way to the church basement to sign up for the open stage, I'd stop at Future Bakery on Bloor Street, at the corner of Brunswick and Bloor. There I'd join a motley group of poets and songwriters sipping teas. I'd have a beer in the hopes of calming my nerves, to keep my hands from clattering with anxiety on the fret of my guitar.

I was influenced by this crew and their penchant for original songs, who proudly shared their offerings each week. I began to figure something out: I had poems, and I already played the guitar.

I might be able to meld the two elements and perhaps write a song or two. Initially, I chanted poetry over song-like clusters of chords, as I had little more than that intuitive idea of the shape of a song — verses, chorus, verse, chorus, bridge — and absolutely no clue how to write melody.

At Fat Albert's (Fat's to those in the community), we'd greet each other with, "What's your number?" "What are you going to play?" We mostly knew each other's repertoire, although I tried to write at least one new song each week. The great songwriter Sam Larkin was there every Wednesday night with a twelve-string guitar and a harmonica in the darkened, womb-like church basement.

"Sally on, let the blood fly where it may," Sam sang. "Sally on and shake the blackened sky just breathing, Sally on, it'll drive you as she walks another way. There is much to be done in the morning." He was brilliant, and even though I was never quite sure what he was on about, he summoned the wind and the sea in his songs, creating a world that I could enter and sit within.

Upon hearing of my pre-performance bakery routine, Sam said, "If you keep that up, you will always need alcohol to play. Stop." I did. Over the next ten years, I went on to write a multitude of songs, record them, lead bands, and play shows across Canada and a few south of the border. Performance never came easily to me, and I was always nervous and could become easily untethered by any suggestion of a need to improvise, or with the requirement that I speak and not just play the songs that I'd written. For some this is as easy as breathing. For me, each gig was hard.

•

On the tour to Montreal, where I'd been hired to play in the band of a small theatre company, I first discovered the difference between actors and musicians. It seemed actors carried imaginary stages in their heads at all times, upon which they were always a central character. In the tour van, they changed seats with great urgency, threw grand, gleeful gestures, flipped accents and tone mid-sentence for improvisatory effect, often while singing. They were always in motion and mostly laughing. The musicians, by contrast — Morgan on bass and David on clarinet, and me — would look dreamily out the window at the passing landscape en route to our next venue, smile occasionally at a particularly raucous actorly witticism. Mostly, we just waited for them to stop.

Our small troupe did two shows per day. Every morning for two weeks, we'd pile into the van in the morning and drive to our first of two high schools, where we'd unload and present our PSA-type show.

During an afternoon of downtime, I decided to challenge myself and busk in the Montreal subway system. In the echoing halls of Berri-UQAM, I strapped on my guitar and placed the empty hard-shell case in front of me. I started to play my original songs, perfected at my weekly forays to Fat Albert's.

A man stopped beside me. He listened intently. At the end of the song, he said, "You're good, but I'm not going to give you any money."

"Why not?"

"Because you don't need it," he said. He'd sized me up — another Caribbean, Black, English speaker with a certain bearing, skin tone, and so on. We do this to each other. He assumed his assessment of me was correct. He imagined that he saw me.

I turned away for a second to put the harmonica holder around my neck. I fixed the harmonica in place. I'd never really learned to play it properly and used it more as a breathy rhythm maker. I turned to look him in the eye. Then, with a brief smile, I blew and strummed an introduction and then sang:

Seven secrets for seven lies
Babylon to Egypt and down the Nile
Climbing back to the place of light
As it was in the beginning
Well, they came and they stole the land,
And said it was at god's command
Well, I know different, 'cause a little bird told me,
something about humanity
Well, they take away your voice and say can't sing, but
that's okay, 'cause little birds whisper
And that little bird, that little broken bird told me
something I'd never heard.
Seven secrets for seven lies ...
We are the survivors of the 100 million diaspora
We are the survivors of the 100 million diaspora
The oldest aesthetic, a true reality, found again in the
red, black and green.
Seven secrets for seven lies ...

"Okay, okay," he said. He put a bill in the case and walked away. Mis-seen, then seen somewhat.

•

The majority of my peers in the Toronto singer/songwriter scene at the time were white. There were a few poets, Bradley and Sahara Sparklin, and songwriters like Bob, Ron, Sam, Cate, Ana, Katherine, Ruthie, Kyp, and the other Bob. The occasional Black person would wander in and stay briefly. Most memorable were Tyrone Gabriel, with his voice of warm wind, only deep, and Jeff Burke, the gentle often-bearded bassoon player who would accompany anyone who asked.

Many of us recorded our songs and released them on cassettes that we traded with each other or tried to place in Sam the Record

Man's indie music section. Before the days of social media, our ads for gigs were 8" x 11" posters copied at Kinkos on Bloor Street and stuck to lampposts with tape.

The first reviews of my recordings were often completely disconnected from what I considered my music to be: pop with a smattering of jazz, folk, and Latin rhythms. One claimed me to be a "Great belting R&B singer." My placement in the line-up of a reggae stage of a prominent Toronto music festival was musically inexplicable. I can only guess that these were written or set up by white reviewers and promoters, and were based on my skin tone and long dreads respectively.

Similar but different scenarios would occur south of the border. In New York City, the following discussion took place with Syd, my Black American music industry contact, who said, "My family would say you a snob."

"Why?" I asked.

"'Cause you talk like that, you talk white."

"I talk like a Canadian," I said. "You need to travel."

I took to Michelle Wright's book, *Physics of Blackness*, with enthusiasm because, in light of such incidents, I feel that she makes space for me. We are many things, are we not? We are not all American when we are Black; we are not all reggae artists if we have dreads. We are complex, and Blackness is so often about place — where we are born, what languages we learned, where and how we move through space. We can exist beyond any dominant presence that tells us how we must fit, what to talk about, how we must write, who we must be.

I remember knowing that I should behave differently, however, I'd developed a kind of perversity from small. I would hide behind my mother's A-line skirt and ransack the peace of morning breakfast. My father, used to giving orders to lower ranks in the military who jumped at his every word, would become apoplectic when I refused to say good morning. His face would crinkle with helpless rage. I would peek out from behind my mother's legs at the scene I had created, refusing the weight of assumptions, the limits of someone else's vision of who I should be. Obedient girl-child. Or more recently, surveilled and limited Blackness.

•

I ran various versions of my band for many years, unaware that my very first guitar teacher had run his own band as well. The Sonny Denner Orchestra played jazz and had also performed and recorded calypso with the Mighty Sparrow in the 1950s. I imagine that Mr. Denner's band stopped when the era of big bands folded. We all change directions. Sometimes a series of clues tell us that it's time to do so.

The smallest gestures let you know that something is not going to work out. Something about moving through space and knowing that extraordinary or even ordinary support is not forthcoming. The Montreal experience, compounded with an overnight sojourn to the Red Dog in Peterborough (where I sang backup in someone else's band), gave me a clear idea of what low-level touring via van through the Canadian landscape might feel like. It might look like long journeys between cities and towns, speakers piled around you and beneath your feet in a small van, most likely with a sea of men. And then there was the work of showing up and possibly being seen, mis-seen, or imagined. Sometimes you just stop.

On that day, the series of events and experiences compounded into one moment. The intention was to complete a second full-length album. It was soon after giving birth, and I was standing in the studio in front of the microphone stand with a five-month-old baby wrapped in a pale blue snuggly slung over my shoulder. As I recall, we recorded some vocals for that session along with some instrumental tracks. The session ended. To get to the other side of town with child and husband involved a bus ride to the subway station. I turned toward the keyboard player who, before I could even get the words out, said, "I don't feel like giving you a ride to the subway." She took her payment and drove away. It was cash, before the days of e-transfers. So, we took the bus, a subway, and then another subway. Okay, I thought. Again. Good reminder. This is what it looks like. You are in an unsupported place. Choose.

Soon after the studio incident, I put down the mantel of band leader with a kind of relief. I sold the Oskar Graf to Kevin Barrett, a great guitar player who reads music with ease, and put the unfinished album in a closet. It seemed like a good route. It felt that to embrace a different life, I might need to softly lay this one down.

Somehow, I want better for young artists. There are few models of how to do this. I received grants but not guidance, and so floundered through the process. Somehow, I want better for mothers who are artists. And even though I did push back at those who would put me in a box, there was the constant issue of feeling simultaneously exposed and unseen, a common thread in my life as a Black woman in the arts. I think I just got tired.

My lessons through music are who I am, though. I don't perform, as I'm too much of a perfectionist to offer my limited playing and voice. I am pleased with exactly three of my many compositions. They are great tunes, perhaps for someone else to sing. And I swear, I am the best audience member ever. I listen from the inside of the process. I understand it all: writing, recording, rehearsing, creating a show, selling merchandise at the door, hoping for a good number of audience members to pay the band or for the right industry person to appear in the crowd or for the best sound engineer for the room. I am also the worst audience member, both knowledgeable and judgemental: Why are the vocals so low in the mix and the guitar so high? It's driving me crazy. Let me at the board. I need to fix this. My ears are burning.

I did pick up the guitar again. Spring 2020 was a critical time for many people. During those first weeks of lockdown, my world was quiet. I now own a nylon-stringed cutaway Godin, a gesture to the memory of the custom-made Oskar Graf. There was space for memory and time for perusing old things. I uncovered some sheet music from my early forays into guitar playing. I re-learned *Chôros No. 1* by Brazilian composer Heitor Villa-Lobos and practised it relentlessly. I thought that I might post a performance in that strange online world of seen/not-seen. Like the doctor–guitar player of my mother's imaginings, it is an interstitial space where we can be as simple or as complex as we wish to be. It is a liminal place where we can be both minute and magnificent. Barefoot, dreaded, wearing a long dress, I placed my nylon-stringed classical guitar on my lap. I felt myself as if back in my quiet childhood bedroom. I looked up, smiled, and played for the camera.

# Trifecta

*And these words are offered in thanks to those who started flames that*
*consumed them as they blazed trails so we are now free to be:*
*Musicians, dancers, thinkers, writers, artists, mystics.*[1]

— Lorna Goodison

Between elementary and graduate school, I attended approximately eight formal institutions of learning. That makes me an expert on delusions and dreams. To make it through various curricula, I suspended disbelief, while hearing what was not being said. I learned to negotiate information that did not include me, the way little Caribbean girls in gingham dresses and bloomers read the adventures of Enid Blyton's Famous Five, not once seeing themselves in the words and sketches, and yet imagining adventures on the moors of England.

Bishop Anstey Junior School was originally an all-girls elementary school. It was founded by the Anglican Bishop Arthur Henry Anstey in 1921, in Trinidad, and like many schools in Anglo-Caribbean islands, followed the colonial British curricula. We wrote compositions about snowy days we'd never seen. We learned calligraphy, writing in italics with flat-nib pens filled from bottles of blue ink, blotting paper close at hand. Exams were sent to England for marking and verification by the originators.

By the time I attended, little boys had been admitted and there had been attempts to incorporate the culture of the island. The music teacher, Miss Yip Choi, brought the cuatro into class. We each were given a four-stringed ukulele-like instrument integral to parang, the music sung in Spanish around Christmas. We learned to pick single notes for the melody of "La Cucaracha," a Mexican folk song.

When I landed in the first of my Canadian schools in Goose Bay, I was well-schooled in the traditions of Empire. I knew the drill. There is always something not said. To exist in these spaces, I accepted absence as normal. The work seemed to be to hold oneself aloft, quietly take in information unrelated to self, and give it back in a neat, concise form. I received great marks and was considered bright.

Next, I attended two schools in North Bay, Ontario: Widdifield High and St. Joseph-Scollard Hall. I attended my final high school in Ottawa, St. Pius X High School, named after a Catholic pope. I graduated from Queen's University in Kingston, Ontario, with a bachelor's degree.

Education in Empire had created for me the belief in reward for good work. Instead, however, in the world of work that followed, this naïveté did not translate well. I found myself languishing in low-level jobs, watching young white women parachuted over me into positions and opportunities that I wanted. In the midst of this persistent debacle, however, I managed to maintain my somewhat contrarian nature, and this is what held me.

•

It was 2019. After plateauing in several government jobs, in a seven-year series of lateral moves, I decided to fully embrace said nature. Turning myself fully over to art, music, and mostly literature, I signed up for a Master of Fine Arts in Creative Nonfiction.

The University of King's College in Halifax, Nova Scotia, is a suite of brick buildings in the northeast corner of the Dalhousie University campus. The two institutes are distinct yet historically connected. I stood in the King's library that June summer day with my MFA cohort. This was our matriculation, the formal ceremony of enrolment into our new centre of learning. The word has its root in "mata" — mother, a tendency or belief in the maternal — mother tongue, motherland, going home, home to the feeling of embrace. However, as I stood there, inside the large sandy-coloured brick building that sits off the courtyard, surrounded by paths and greenery, I felt not embraced but perched in an English fantasy world that linked seamlessly with my Trinidad schooling in Empire, where I'd been dressed in a gingham uniform and bloomers.

Before us stood William Lahey, the president of the university. He wore a black cap with a gold tassel and what looked like a red cape over a formal suit. He stood between busts of two Greek men, and above him hovered the winged, armless, headless torso of a woman. He told us the two men were Greek statesmen, Cicero and Demosthenes. The winged, headless, armless torso was called the *Winged Victory of Samothrace*. She was also called the goddess Nike.

One by one we were called to sign our names into the registry of all who had ever studied at this place. I felt extremely uncomfortable. I realized I was having a disembodied and frightening experience, different from that of most of my excited peers. I wondered if anyone else who looked like me, who shared any of my histories, had stood in this place. How many Black, brown, or Indigenous people had signed their names into this book? In a moment of panic, I wondered if this was even a desirable thing to do. I turned to consider the exit. I turned back to the room, undecided.

I thought back to breakfast earlier that morning, in Prince Hall. I'd looked around at the oil paintings of white men that covered the walls twenty feet above my head. I sliced my bagel and placed it in the toaster, and went to the nook that held fridges and hot food to get oat milk for my coffee. After four Canadian high schools and one university campus, this demographic scenario was not new to me, however, this time, my experience was different.

We were now in the midst of an overt racial reckoning with the Black Lives Matter movement. I did not yet know this, but since 2015, there had been incidents of "anti-Black racial/overt racial incidents" on this very campus. The Black faculty and staff caucus at Dalhousie University had already met with the university's president, Dr. Richard Florizone, and chair of the Dalhousie Senate, Dr. Kevin Hewitt, to discuss racism and university campus life. They'd already discussed omissions and biases in the curriculum and a general lack of professional progress for Black professors. They'd already sought the roots of silences and quiet violence, hidden except to those experiencing them. I did not know, by the time I showed up to stand in ceremony, that "the Report" had already been researched and written.

Awareness of this might have helped my general orientation to the environment and campus. It might have put me in touch with someone — Black students, history, context, understanding — and I might not have felt so dissociated. Instead, I stood alone, the sole Black person in my cohort — unmoored. The building itself felt hostile. Isolated and confused, I held myself emotionally apart from the others. We shared a space, but I felt myself part of a different ceremony. Among the bodies present, I could see and feel breath beside me; I heard and felt the incorporeal reach through time. At University of King's College, in that moment, standing in the library surrounded by humans, I was listening to ghosts. I felt spectres drift out of the walls and make their presence known.

There are photos of me standing on the steps of the library after the matriculation. In one, I am alone. A black gown covers my yellow-and-black ankle-length summer dress. I recall the comforting sway of it in the gentle breeze, soft against my bare legs. Another photo is with my assigned mentor group. The five of us link arms. I grin for the camera.

•

The year before starting my MFA, I'd spent six weeks in Salvador, Bahia, Brazil. Just off the Praça da Sé, in the Museum of Mercy, a security guard remained about ten feet away from me at all times. He wore a beatific open smile and a machine gun. My tour guide, a young Black man, was angry and embarrassed. He told me there were cameras everywhere and that the guard was being directed to follow me, a Black woman, through an earpiece. In response, he gave me a tour I was probably not supposed to get.

"Look at those paintings." He pointed to a series of seventeeth-century oils of Portuguese men taking part in a procession. Each man was holding up a painting of one of the Stations of the Cross. It was obviously night time.

"Why do you think we can see the paintings that they are holding up?" he challenged me. Then, caught up in his own frustration, he quickly answered his own question.

"Because they were surrounded by people holding up lamps. Slaves were holding up lamps. The slaves are not in the picture. Or in the museum." He pointed in disgust to two lamps on six-foot poles leaning against a back wall, the only reference to the existence of people who had made the event visible that night.

A year later, in the King's library, I stood in another institute full of silences and shadows. I wondered whose hands had cut stone, dug foundations, and built this campus. What narrative is upheld and which parallel ones were omitted? Who was holding up the lamps to light the university, an apparent beacon of learning and elucidation?

●

It seems there was a team of light bearers already at work. Among them was Dr. Afua Cooper, lead author of the 2019 "Report on Lord Dalhousie's History on Slavery and Race." She and a panel of academics had delved into the history of the university's namesake, Lord Dalhousie, his associations, and his personal and professional history.

The report is devastating. It reveals the deep human cost of the university's creation and maintenance, as well as the complicity of the social infrastructure that surrounds it. In addition to being built on stolen Indigenous land and resources, the area had built its wealth via the enslavement of Black people and a highly developed, triangulated trade that linked the Caribbean, Canada, and Europe. Goods made by enslaved people in the Caribbean where shipped north. The Atlantic coast's salted cod was shipped south to feed enslaved people. The report traces the legacy of such a core foundation, its impact on our society today and on campus life.

My new alma mater, originally called King's Collegiate School, was founded in 1788 in Windsor, Nova Scotia. "Since the late 1980s, the University of King's College has claimed to be a successor institution to the original King's College in New York."[2] In

2017, King's College, now called Columbia University, released an investigation and a report into its deep roots and the origins of some of its wealth through the enslavement of Black people.

King's Collegiate School in Windsor burned to the ground in 1920. It was rebuilt with financial support from Dalhousie University in a corner of its campus in 1922. The institute's pursuit of research and their own connections to slavery triggered a closer look by King's.

"Inquiry into the history of King's relative to slavery has another important rationale. It is that King's cannot hope to be viewed as a welcoming community to people of African descent unless it openly and forthrightly addresses the questions that can legitimately be asked about its history in relation to people of African descent, including its history relative to the history of slavery in Nova Scotia,"[3] wrote one of the report's authors.

No wonder I felt unmoored.

Martinique is one of an arc of tiny islands that arise out of the Caribbean Sea. It sits between Dominica in the north and Saint Lucia in the south. Starting in the fifteenth century, European nations invaded and parcelled out the islands among themselves, giving them such names. Sometimes they would fight among themselves and then the islands would change hands. Initially, the French took Martinique. As a rule, however, regardless of nationality, the Europeans slaughtered the Kalinago, the Taino, and other original peoples of the Caribbean islands. In the next stage of terror, Africans were kidnapped and shipped in to clear and plant the lush green lands in the "organized violence" of agricultural forced labour camps, a supremely apt term coined by Samuel P. Huntington in *The Clash of Civilizations and the Remaking of World Order*.

This is where Canada's Dalhousie (the title Lord came later) received some early training in the maintenance of Empire. On the island of Martinique, with firepower and guns, violence and torture, he helped to re-enslave people who had freed themselves, in tandem with the revolutionary movement and social upheaval that was taking place in France.

Soon after these acts, Dalhousie would be named the new lieutenant governor of Nova Scotia to govern the British colony from 1816 to 1820.

> Dalhousie's arrival coincided with the recent migration to and settlement in Nova Scotia of the Black Refugees of the War of 1812. They had come from the southern United States, namely the Chesapeake region and parts of coastal Georgia. As former enslaved persons, the Black Refugees had supported the British Crown in its fight against the United States in the newly ended war.[4]

Dalhousie had come to Nova Scotia with his training techniques and philosophy of vicious racism intact. In his new assignment (it seemed a promotion), Lord Dalhousie was supported by a society and culture that had oppressed Indigenous people and was ensconced on their land. With regards to people of African descent who fled to or were brought there, he was deeply engaged in ensuring their lives were untenable. The arrivants[5] were placed on un-arable land, with little of the financial support provided to white settlers. Dalhousie referred to Black people as unworthy of freedom. In fact, some people were sent back into slavery in the West Indies, to the island of Trinidad where emancipation had not yet taken place.

Meanwhile, the province's coffers grew fat due to a robust trade to and from the Caribbean. Food was shipped south to feed enslaved populations, and quantities of rum and molasses were shipped north. Shipbuilding, insurance companies, and other associated industries developed in support of a lucrative trade in goods made by unpaid labour. Indeed, the report found that the university had been funded by such trade. And yes, indeed, via connections to Dalhousie University, the buildings of my new alma mater were deeply shaped by the hands and wealth built from the labour of people who looked very much like me and, due to the Trinidad connection, were quite possibly some of my people.

·

In the noisy and jubilant post-lockdown gatherings at Kensington Market, Toronto, writer and academic Jacqueline Scott and I look for a quiet place to talk. I spot a promising outdoor patio just off the main drag where two customers sit at one of six tables. The exuberant worker behind the counter brings us our coffees. Then the usual. She puts on some dancehall music and raises the volume in increments while checking us repeatedly for reaction. Evidently, this is what two Black women with dreads want to hear at this very moment. Is she hoping for a nod of approval, for an imagined solidarity with us? We sigh, pack up, and go in search of another location. At a perch outdoors on a low wooden barrier at the edge of a parking lot on Bellevue Avenue, I pull out my recorder and I ask her about absence.

Schooled in Jamaica, England, and Canada, all three points of a triangulated trade, she has direct experience in the variety of obfuscations enacted by Empire. Each society supported the other's version of an ahistorical and disposable people: those of African descent brought to the islands as chattel, indentured Indians and Asians and people indigenous to continents and islands of the Americas. In effect, numerous peoples remained incomplete, obscure, shadowy tales.

"I experienced different kinds of absence and invisibility. They reinforce each other, in that you remain outside of history, not present in the progression of humanity. In elementary school in Jamaica, I experienced a cognitive disconnect, in that I could see myself in all areas of society, up to the leadership; however, we were given Dick and Jane readers and asked to write an essay on a snowy day in England. We were quizzed relentlessly on the names of Columbus's ships, the *Nina*, the *Santa Maria*, and the *Pinta*," she laughs.

In England: "We're giving you the best English education, but we're not seeing you as a Black person, so therefore, when you have issues with race, you don't have the language to express what is going on. You are supposed to be grateful, but then, why are the skinheads waiting for me outside of the school gate? These things are hard to spot or name when you're in the middle of it and don't have the language to ask for what is missing. The first time I saw a book written by a Black person was in university. I asked a professor about African empires. He told me 'there weren't any as it was too hot.' Huge swaths of humanity and experiences were just not there."

In Canada, Jacqueline is completing her PhD. Here, it manifests differently, she tells me. The title of her thesis is *Black Outdoors: The Perception of Wilderness in the Canadian Imagination*. She studies hiking, camping, and the presence or absence of Black Canadians in these spaces.

"There is an insane level of rigour, referencing that Black, Indigenous, and basically all scholars who are people of colour face. When I make a statement, any statement, it requires an insane level of referencing. White PhDs don't have to do this level of referencing. But the Black PhD student does. This is how racism works in academia. I naively expected academia to be different because, it's like, wow, we are the ones who are creating knowledge. We're the ones who are shaping the world. I lost heart for a while, when I realized that it's racism, and I actually have to work twice as hard, like all the other Black PhD students, because our work is 'not objective.' Those are coded ways of undermining what you are doing. I'm dealing with the stress of almost having to insist that my research is legitimate, that it is worthy of a PhD, that I have something to say that has profound implications."

•

In 2003, Ruth J. Simmons, the first African American president of Brown University, an Ivy League institution, commissioned the *Report of the Brown University Steering Committee on Slavery and Justice*. The report triggered the activation of new policies at the university and inspired the development of Universities Studying Slavery, "a consortium of over ninety institutions of higher learning in the United States, Canada, Colombia, Scotland, Ireland, and England. These schools are focused on sharing best practices and guiding principles as they engage in truth-telling educational projects focused on human bondage and the legacies of racism in their histories."[6]

*Ebony and Ivy: Race, Slavery, and the Troubled History of America's Universities*, written by Craig Steven Wilder, a historian and professor at the Massachusetts Institute of Technology, focuses on the connections between many American academic institutions in the United States and slavery and the use of slave labour. Wilder did not stop with the U.S., however, and notes how these mechanisms exist in other former colonies such as those found in Latin America, the Caribbean, and Canada. In 2017, Dalhousie University became the first Canadian university to join the consortium.

On the very first page of Wilder's book, he outlines how the structures of colonialism and education were linked and dependent upon each other:

The founding, financing, and development of higher education in the colonies were thoroughly intertwined with the economic and social forces that transformed West and Central Africa through the slave trade and devastated indigenous nations in the Americas. The academy was a beneficiary and defender of these processes.[7]

[...]

Colleges were imperial instruments akin to armories and forts, a part of the colonial garrison with the specific responsibilities to train ministers and missionaries, convert Indigenous people and soften cultural resistance, and extend European rule over foreign nations.[8]

Canadian universities do indeed have deep links to African chattel slavery, and the Dalhousie report listed many examples I was unaware of:

- The University of New Brunswick named its law school after pro-slavery Judge George Ludlow. On two occasions, as Supreme Court judge, Ludlow returned two enslaved Black people to their owners whereas these Black people had sued for their freedom.
- McGill University was founded from an endowment from James McGill, a wealthy Scottish-born Montreal fur trader and entrepreneur. McGill bought and sold enslaved Africans and also kept enslaved persons in bondage.

- Jesuit-supported schools, like Saint Mary's University, Campion, Loyola, and Regis Colleges are linked to Jesuit institutions that were major slaveholders in the United States and Latin America.
- Laval University is also linked to enslavement through its missionizing activities among Indigenous peoples in Quebec and other parts of Canada.
- Additionally, Joseph Allison, the grandfather of Charles Frederick Allison, the founder of Mount Allison University, was a slave owner.
- To this group can be added University of Toronto, which was originally founded as King's College by High Church Anglicans. As is now known, the Anglican Church has had close imbrications with the transatlantic slave trade and colonial slavery itself.
- When Dalhousie College was founded, it received its original endowment from the Castine Fund. This fund consisted of customs duties charged on the imports of goods entering Castine, Maine, during the time Britain occupied the territory. A substantial part — 30 per cent — of these duties were charged on slave-made goods from the West Indies. The British government made these funds available to the lieutenant-governor of Nova Scotia to spend.[9]

*Ebony and Ivy* and the *Report* were both emotionally challenging reads on complex and deliberate mechanisms. The enslavement of others, along with trade in goods made using free labour, is a deeply integrated system that created wealth all over the Americas and Europe. Educational and religious systems were integral parts of it. I knew all of this on some level, but reading and studying these truths and their conscious implementation and the integration of such mechanisms made me feel ill.

●

My general modus operandi and coping strategy to date for moving through Empire has been to try to make it through the absences, obfuscations, lies, and violence, and to come out the other side somewhat intact; to make it through the ever-present borders, metaphysical or actual; to just get the certificate or the experience or the contacts and find my way back home to my box in the sky, paycheque or degree in hand.

Some people become still when distressed. They try meditation, prayer, and the like. I need to move.

At a dance workshop in Toronto, a group of about twenty-five people are under the tutelage of Cuban dancer Dailyn Martinez. Percussionist Magdelys Savigne, also Cuban, has joined and sits on a raised stage. She plays and sings in concert with the teachings.

Martinez teaches us movements from the Arará tradition (Ewe-Fon of Dahomey, now Benin), a minority community in the mostly Yoruba pantheon in Cuba. The religion and its movements were brought by enslaved people, in their bodies, memories, and spirit, as they were shipped across the Atlantic from Africa to the Americas.

One dance we learn is the characteristic movements of Asojano (Babalú Ayé in another Afro-Cuban tradition). This entity is a bearer of both disease and healing. He makes a scratching motion with the hand, on alternating shoulders; his feet stomp as he moves forward, his shoulders and chest undulate. In the same motion, he withdraws his fingernails and flattens his hand to stroke the body in the transmission of healing, as he calms the body, the mind, the spirit.

There are alternate stories in the ether for me to catch.

I take a break from reading various reports to acknowledge disease, to move, to scratch it off and to heal, to dance Asojano. I brush off the diseased thoughts that created slavery. I cleanse the impact they've had on me as I read this today. I brush it off my left shoulder and then the right. I move my feet to the syncopated timing of Arará. I round and fling my shoulders back, pulse my chest forward, back as if I were moving wings on my back. I am flying around this evil for a moment. I brush it off and then I circle back in, fly to my stool at the kitchen counter, to the beastly and brilliant documents that await me. I pick one up and keep reading.

•

At the start of the report, Professor Afua Cooper has written a note. It begins with a poem.

> babalawos emerge from the storm
> divining with their shells and stones[10]

Then she writes:

> The Nova Scotia Human Rights Commission's
> *Halifax, Nova Scotia, Street Checks Report*, written
> by criminologist Scott Wortley, informs us that
> Black people in Halifax, especially Black men,
> are six times more likely to be street checked by
> police than white people. Black people are there-
> fore singled out by police officers in practices that
> are racist and discriminatory. This is particularly
> alarming given they make up only 3.59% of the

city's population. The Dalhousie Report gives res-
onance to the "Street Checks Report" in that it
provides the historical basis for the current condi-
tion of Blacks in Halifax with respect to this particular discriminatory exercise. Many, if not most,
of the Black Haligonians who are street checked
are descendants of the Black Refugees of the War
of 1812 and Caribbean and African immigrants.[11]

Cooper links the policies of Lord Dalhousie's government and
Nova Scotia's previous and successive administrations that ensured
"the philosophy of history, knowledge and education, and it brings
to bear the realization that history, especially that of Black people,
is oftentimes erased and deliberately so.... The Black Refugees were
relegated to a caste-like environment that normalized social con-
scription and educational and political marginalization."[12]

I've often wondered about the deliberate and purposeful omission of stories. The most often repeated narrative of Canada is that
of the land of freedom, when in fact many Black people were enslaved or lived here under brutal conditions. At times, Black people
fled Canada and went back to the U.S., where their children could
be free under different laws.

Some people fled in another direction. "In 1792, twelve hundred Black Loyalists fled Nova Scotia in a flotilla of fifteen ships
to sail from Halifax, Nova Scotia, to Freetown, Sierra Leone," says
author Lawrence Hill in an interview on his research for *The Book
of Negroes*, a novel based on the early history of people of African
descent in Canada. "This back-to-Africa exodus took place more
than a century before the famed Jamaican Marcus Garvey urged
Blacks in the Diaspora to return to the motherland. It took place
decades before people formerly enslaved in America founded
Liberia. The first massive back-to-Africa exodus in world history

set off from the shores of Halifax, but to date, few Canadians know it."[13]

The panel clarified the links between slavery, the university, society in general, and links to anti-Black racism today. Halifax was one of the cornerstones of the triangulated trade in coffee, sugar, molasses, and rum between the islands of the Caribbean Sea, South America, and Europe.

And yes, these goods had funded the stones of the campus, the walls within which I stood. The world that surrounded me. A triangulated, deeply established, and invisible, or at least unrecognized, system had enriched the university's coffers, contributed to building the infrastructure and possibly its very walls. Individuals at Dalhousie University were holding up a light to sordid connections and "the role that academies played in maintaining racial hierarchies and embedded anti-Blackness."[14]

One of the report's researchers, Shirley Tillotson, published an essay, "How (and how much) King's College benefited from slavery in the West Indies, 1789 to 1854." Tillotson writes, "Between 1803 and 1833, I find that 35.7 per cent of the public funding to King's in those years came from taxes on slave-produced goods." She goes on to state, "We inherit an institution funded at its origin by unjustly extracted profits and taxes charged on blood-soaked goods. We should understand the benefit to the College and the province that was taken from enslaved people of the 18th and 19th century West Indies."[15]

•

I don't know what the response was from other Canadian universities to the existence of such research. I do know that in her book *They Said This Would Be Fun*, Eternity Martis shares her experiences from her time on campus at the University of Western Ontario, revealing a skewed culture of racism and exclusion.

The University of Western Ontario was also my father's alma mater, where he'd studied medicine in the late 1950s. He did not tell us what he'd experienced as the only Black medical student. I envisioned considerable challenges in that environment. He did tell us that he made friends, had some great peers, and was voted valedictorian by his classmates. A year after his death in 2021, I received an email from Dr. Michael Hunter, one of those same classmates, class of '63:

> The alumni office of the Medical School has asked me if I could help them in contacting any of Steve's family members as the Dean apparently wants to honour him with an "Alumni of Distinction Award." Our class nominated Steve for this several years ago, but only recently have the "powers-that-be" come to consider our proposal. If my amateur sleuthing has been correct and you are his daughter.

When we spoke on the phone, Hunter's tone was clear. He and his classmates had nominated my father for an alumni award years before he'd died and nothing had happened.

"If you want to follow up, here is the email address of those who want to get in touch with your family. I'm sorry this is so late. Your choice."

My mother's response was along the lines of, enough awards already, it's kind of late, can we talk about something else?

And of course, I could not help but analyze the timing of the request following so closely behind Eternity Martis's highly successful book. Perhaps some reputation repair was needed, or a crisis of conscience had occurred. A need to fill in absences with recognition and the need for some Black faces on walls, and such. We know how this works. I've seen so many Black and brown faces on bank ads in the past two years. Was this a public relations impulse toward an appearance of remediation without systemic change?

The next call came from the Canadian Medical Hall of Fame. What is going on here? I asked myself. I knew, but still I felt the need to ask myself out loud. Are there any other Black doctors in there, I wonder, or is this collect-some-Black-folk-for-the-wall season? Had my father just been discovered by his own alma mater and the Canadian medical establishment, two years after his death? I was pissed and did my best to be gracious for my own sake and that of any interlocutors.

I thought of my older brother, who often says, "Thanks for the awards. Where's the money?"

Professor Kevin Hewitt, chair of the Dalhousie Senate and one of the primary supporters of the initiative, says differently.

> My own ancestry connects my maternal great-grandmother Daisy Louisa Forde (née Williams), born June 1885, to her father, Joseph Williams, born a couple decades earlier in St. Vincent and the Grenadines. Joseph was the son of parents from Grenada enslaved by the British. Imagine the exploitation of these human beings, the goods produced by their unpaid and coerced labour and how it enriched others both near and far. How did this legacy of enslavement affect not only this family, but the wider Black population in the Atlantic littoral? How has this enslavement and marginalization affected how we and others are perceived? What of their socio-economic life trajectories and that of their children and their

children's children? What is owed to these individuals and their descendants for a systemic op-
pression that denied them their humanity? What
could possibly compensate them for their treat-
ment as moveable chattel — property listed in
wills, sale ads, and estate records alongside furniture and farm animals?[16]

•

Did I mention that I am lucky? That my parents were schooled,
became solidly middle class. My brothers and I were educated in
Empire, our grandparents were teachers. That even among stone
castles that store and repeat truncated and maligned histories, I'm
here. My mother quotes Wordsworth at ninety-two:

> I wandered lonely as a cloud
> That floats on high o'er vales and hills,
> When all at once I saw a crowd,
> A host, of golden daffodils;
> Beside the lake, beneath the trees,
> Fluttering and dancing in the breeze.

She learned this as a child at Tranquility Elementary School in
Trinidad. From her I learned to love words. Even if they were often
about daffodils and such.

Did I mention that I am fortunate? I had a profound, parallel
education all along the way. I swallowed it whole, undigested,
as easy as air. My formal schooling was accompanied by never-
ending exposure to art and music. In my parents' home, along
with medical texts and endless documentaries on military jets
and flying, music was writ large. The analysis, commentary,
wisdom, and driving joy of calypso surrounded us, as did my

father's prodigious collection of Cuban music, American jazz, and the music of Brazil. These complex rhythms and melodies, and their connection to dance held eras, histories, resistance, and more.

Did I say that we, my family and I, should not be possible?

Among my formal references is an experience once again had while in Brazil. In 2018, I attended the funeral of Mestre King, a dancer, historian, and choreographer of Afro-Brazilian dance, and a specialist in Orixá dance movement. I met a multitude of his students and mentees. Some called him a university, as he carried and transmitted eras through teaching dance, where information can be embodied. The wave of a hand at a certain angle implies an archetype, references a pantheon and all the stories attached to it.

At Dodem Kanonhsa' in Toronto, I was exposed to another wisdom. That day, First Nations Elder Clayton Shirt held a circle. At one point, the dialogue and questions had focused on the separation between cultures. This caused me deep distress, as like many people of the Caribbean, I knew of my multiple heritages (African, Indian, Kalinago, and various Europeans). "How are we all the same? I need to know. How we are all the same?" I insisted. He answered with this: "We all come with the same original instructions."

I have held these words close to me for decades since.

Those words also said to me that we, humans, know when we do wrong. We know when we are looking askance, are choosing to not see our complicity, particularly when the spoils of these behaviours remain in plain sight.

Historian Dr. Charmaine Nelson revealed evidence of Canadian slavery in newspapers where "owners" advertised for the return of "lost property" or "runaway slaves." She also brought awareness to the vestiges of the slave trade that remain in Canadian culture today.

Nova Scotian liquor stores are stocked with more rum than, say, a Saskatchewan liquor store because of the cultural holdover from those 1800s merchant ships, which brought scads of the stuff to our port — along with other plantation crops and enslaved peoples. People just look at it like, "Oh, this is just how we are." Like, really? Why do you think that is?[17]

History surrounds us if we choose to notice — in ordinary objects, turns of phrase, objects, food, liquor. And if we all come with the same original instructions, it also means, to me, that we know when we can do better, different.

Afua Hirsch writes for the *Guardian*: "In 2017, All Souls College at Oxford launched an annual scholarship for Caribbean students and paid a £100,000 grant to a college in Barbados, in recognition of its funding from Christopher Codrington, a wealthy slave owner who bequeathed £10,000 in 1710 to build a library that bears his name."[18]

In the same article, we learn that in 2019, the University of Glasgow, Scotland, committed to "giving" (giving back?) £20 million to the University of the West Indies. Hirsch quotes Graham Campbell, a Scottish National party councillor of African-Caribbean descent: "Our mutual recognition of the appalling consequences of that past — an indictment of Scottish inhumanity over centuries towards enslaved Africans — are the justifications that are at the root of the modern-day racism that we fight now. This action is a necessary first step in the fight against institutionalised racism and discrimination in Scotland and the U.K. and for the international fight for reparative justice."[19]

•

Absence is a thing that I hold, like a being, like a breath. I bring it into space to be looked at and held, to be spoken or sung. I am writing to avoid omission, lost voices, and another disappeared experience. I am writing this for us. I mark us down.

I, too, was schooled in and quizzed on the names of the trifecta of the ships of doom. Now, my trifecta is memory, art, and divination. So that instead of swaying unmoored by the absence, I hold onto the walls and listen to stones.

When I return to Halifax to attend my father's inauguration into the Canadian Medical Hall of Fame, I may revisit the Dalhousie University campus. I will think of my previous schools: Bishops Junior, Bishops High, Goose High, Widdifield High, St. Joe's, St. Pius X, Queen's University. I will think of my parents, grandparents, great-grandparents, and the ones whose names disappeared during the forced journey to the Americas. I will think about how someone else dreamed those buildings and educational institutions, how they were not meant for us, how we showed up anyway. Sometimes we got something out of what they had on offer, sometimes nothing or barely enough to continue. Sometimes, miraculously, regardless, we thrived.

I may visit the library at the University of King's College with more strength and knowledge this time round. This time, I will look at the headless, armless, voiceless statue of a possibly white woman (we don't know as all the paint came off the original, perhaps she was brown like the people of that region at that time, brown like me), and I will think of all the poems I've read, the dances I've learned, the music I've listened to and played, and the degrees in my pocket.

I won't look in dismay at the mutated torso in a place of honour in the King's library. Instead, I will run these names in my head as I walk toward it, the names of some of those who inform me still. Merle LaBorde Blizzard, Lillian Allen, Afua Hirsch,

Lorna Goodison, M. NourbeSe Philip, Lee Maracle, Michelle M. Wright, Charmaine Nelson, Rosangela Silvestre, Isabel Wilkerson, Camille Turner, Jacqueline L. Scott, Sara Ahmed, Sarah Schulman, Deborah Levy, Mayra Caridad Valdés — Chucho's invisible genius sister. I will also hear in my mind the voices of the ones who did not get to speak — the women, men, all beings with heads, minds, voices ... and wings.

# Water

*... the strangest people in the world are those people recognized be-neath one's senses, by one's soul — the people utterly indispensable for one's journey.*

— James Baldwin, *Just Above My Head*

One day, without notice to myself, or lessons of any kind, suddenly, I could swim. I was seven. It was as if a memory of some internal amniotic instructions had arisen within me. That day, I went to a party in the hills at the home of a very rich person, or rather the party of a child with parents who had a grand Trinidad mountainside home. I remember that among the clatter and the laughter and the splashing around of the other girls, I calmly entered the slight chill of blue chlorinated water, floated, and then paddled, head held high above the surface. I was fully at ease with myself, immersed and comfortable, pleased and smiling. Within a year or so, after my parents provided formal swimming lessons, I had joined a competitive swim team, swam my first mile, and saved my baby brother from drowning.

This might be a story of grace. It might be a story of saving others and being saved over and over again — by a shadow, an essence, a person, a scenario. It might be a story of the power of water. It might be a story of how water holds, intertwined, cross-continental memories, or how it activates a dormant seed of emotion. Or it might just be a story of amniotic instructions in an oft-repeated first breath. Life, it seems, is a sequence of near-drownings, rising to the surface, and falling again.

•

I first heard Cesária Évora's voice in my twenties and, as I was already lost, decided that I was from wherever her voice originated. I could hear within it the sea, sadness, longing, and joy and I wanted to be in the company of such things. I wanted to linger and swim within her lustrous voice. I may not have liked her if I'd known her, but I did love her. Knowing nothing of its tumultuous history, for a time I wanted to be Cabo Verdean, to belong to a place that could produce such wondrous sounds.

Years later, on a winter night in 2003, I made my way down to Massey Hall on Victoria Street to hear Cesária Évora sing. I was on my own that night, as no one in my then circle of friends knew who she was. I'd made such a mistake before, not going to see Oscar Peterson one November because no one would come with me. I imagined I'd catch him on the next tour. I was not going to miss Cesária, because of weather, lack of a sidekick, or any other reason. I climbed the steep stairs to my seat in the balcony, sat on the hard chair there, and leaned forward, toward the stage.

Next to me was a woman from St. Catharines who had driven to Toronto that afternoon for the concert. No one in her world knew who Cesária was either, and regardless, she'd driven for two hours, compelled to be here.

Cesária had surrounded herself with the best musicians, and I could tell that she was exacting as they watched her with great attention. I felt she would have heard any error and would have stopped proceedings to fix it.

On the tour to support the album *Voz d'Amor*, Antonio Domingos Gomes Fernandes played the soprano sax. I recognize where the weight sits in the phrase in his lilting syntax. It sits well within me, like the kaiso phrasing imbibed in my childhood surroundings in Trinidad. The violin and saxophone played like waves falling and tumbling skillfully over and past each other, overlapping like dancers that touch and then dive playfully away. Notes like countless streaming fingertips caressed my ears. The elegant band also included the melodic and harmonic density of two guitars, piano, cavaquinho, and bass.

The band would have started the night without the singer, playing "Nutridinha," a word that translates roughly as "a fine woman." And then, the diva would have arrived. She would have worn a long dress, walked to centre stage in her side-to-side gait, barefoot. A stagehand would have given her the microphone.

She would have sung some more coladeras. Mostly, she would have sung mornas, the song tradition that holds longing, regret, sadness, and sodade, a word that is barely translatable into English that holds both bitterness and sweet, joy, and the missing of those who have travelled far away.

Next to me during the concert, the woman from St. Catharines fed me mints when my throat started to tickle and I coughed. It was a beautiful moment of comfort, as my mother used to carry the same spherical white candy. Now a stranger fed them to me at a

Cesária Évora concert. I was in a kind of heaven as I swam within the voice, such lustrous music and care.

"Nha cancera ka tem medida," my fatigue is immesasurable, sings Évora.

For a time, Évora, tired of working and sharing her genius and still not making enough to buy food or a home for her family, suffered deep depression. For ten years, she did not sing regularly. Later, while she was in France, a Paris-based Cabo Verdean brought her out into the spotlight. Like most of us, her life has contained a cycle of near-drownings and salvation.

•

During childhood in Port of Spain, Trinidad, my younger brother, Carlos, and I were at the YMCA pool where I'd recently swam the seventy-two laps that made up my first mile. This was recreation swim time, however, and while I dove in and out of the deep end, I kept an eye on my five-year-old brother as he practised his new skill. He floated on his back and kicked, making a glorious splashing sound. His head would dart in random directions with the effort of pumping his little feet. Then he'd stand, jumping in the shallow water, wiping chlorinated water from his eyes and nose. As I knew that he did not yet know how to swim, I checked to see if the lifeguard was watching him. She was about fourteen, sitting with her back against the concrete pool house, scanning the waters. I caught her eye, then looked at my brother. Her gaze did not follow mine, her head moving slowly up and down the length of the pool. Then my brother was on his back again, head definitively pointed toward deep waters, and he was kicking hard.

I knew that in seconds he would be vertical, his legs trying to touch the bottom. When he moved to stand, I saw the look on his face, the lack of ground beneath him registering. He flailed. I raced toward him in the fastest front crawl that my eight-year-old self could muster. As I reached him, he grabbed me around the neck and squeezed, his legs curled around my chest. I could not breathe. We both sank below the surface.

When my feet touched the bottom, I pulled at his arms as he unwittingly strangled me, and then pushed off the pool's cement floor as hard as I could. I would repeat this desperate routine — pull his arms from my neck, jump, breathe in, sink, pull his arms from my neck, jump, breathe in, sink. By now, my brother had manoeuvred himself onto my back, legs around my torso, arms still at my neck. Beneath my feet, I could feel the concrete slanting upward. I knew somehow that if I could push up on an angle, leaning in that direction, I could move us closer to the shallow end.

As soon as I could stand, I untangled his arms from my neck and pulled him to the pool's edge. He scrambled and I pushed, and then he was on the deck, breathing rapidly, coughing and wiping his face. I looked immediately to the lifeguard. She'd seen nothing, still slowly turning her head mechanically from side to side, as if scanning the water in a performance of life-guarding.

•

Over the last few years, I have been busy saving myself. This included going on my first writing retreat in a decade or so. The long road that led south to the Caribbean coast of Costa Rica, Central America, cut through city, rural villages, and swaths of jungle. Volcanoes sat within view on both sides of the road. My travelling partner and I learned that this was a trucking route for agriculture, that behind those trees was a port, and down that road lay Universidad EARTH. Our driver, Walter, informed us that "this is the most dangerous road in Costa Rica." We were not sure if that last detail was useful.

When we eventually reached a spot of road where we could see the Caribbean Sea through the trees, I sat up. I had touched a lake in Ajijic, Mexico, swam in the ocean off the coast of Salvador, Brazil. These were portals to memories, but not the thing itself. Now, I had again arrived at my Caribbean Sea of childhood. It took exactly this long to return.

•

My friend and I are staying in mountainous terrain a few minutes' walk from the water. Ubuntu Jungle Home Retreat is a two-storey, two-bedroom casita, run by d'bi.young, another Canadian. The soundscape is new to me. On the first night there are thumps of fruit landing on the ground. I hear animals rustling, strange yowls, objects (most likely more fruit) slamming onto the aluminum roof. Once my being calms and my ears adjust, I can hear the relentless roar of the sea. Early the next morning, we clamber down the hill to the black sands beach. In the water, a few metres from shore, is the wreck of a building or perhaps a ship. For now, I will imagine it is a ship — an abandoned ship that once carried people from one part of the world to here.

A shaman once told me to make an offering whenever I meet a new body of water. I am re-meeting the Caribbean seas after travelling far away, bodily, emotionally, psychically. This time, I am here with agency and by choice. I follow my prescription, make my offering of milk. It dribbles from the white-and-blue carton onto my hand and into the sea. I pour milk-blood into the sea for myself, for my Africans, for my Kalinago, and my Indians. Do I pour for my Europeans? Yes, they have suffered a contraction of spirit that they are still overcoming. The offering is a greeting, an acknowledgement, a thank-you — a landing that joins points around the Black Atlantic psychically, emotionally, bodily, activating links and lineages.

On day three of my Costa Rica retreat, I sit at Cunha's Kitchen, a tiny restaurant noticeable from the street only by the huge Rasta flag pitched toward the road. The owner, Cunha, a tiny woman in a colourful head wrap, is originally from Nicaragua. She speaks to me in Spanish with a few words of English, and I determine to get my Spanish language skills together for the next trip. She is making a "Lee Scratch" shake for me, a mix of mango, jackfruit, banana, orange, and yogourt. Other shakes on the menu read like Jamaican music royalty: Marcia Griffiths, Peter Tosh, Bob and Rita Marley. I go to wait in the small seating area behind the green wooden fence.

I hear calypso coming from Cunha's small sound system. Matthew, dreaded like me, hovers nearby, ready either for contact or no contact. So I speak. "Esta música é do meu país," I say in the English-accented Brazilian Portuguese lodged in my brain, which refuses to give way to Spanish despite my efforts. He looks at me sideways and responds in Jamaican-accented English. He tells me of his history on this land. Following the abolition of slavery in Jamaica in 1838, many people migrated to Costa Rica, where there was work building the country's infrastructure, railroads, and ports. Matthew's grandmother travelled here to bake and sell bread to the workers. "A likkle hustle, you know." I smile at the slight tilt of his head as he says this. And then he adds, "You and me, we are the same people. Same music, same history, same food, same t'ing." So many leavings and arrivals. I think again of morna while I sit near these diasporic seas.

· · ·

In our mothers' bodies, our cozy amniotic sac, the fetus is 99 percent water. We are 90 percent water at birth. Seventy percent as an adult. This decreases as we age to around 50 percent. Drink water, my friends. We carry via water within us energy, nutrients, and information. The ocean is a place where we can imagine being mostly water and sit within planetary memories held in its roiling molecular structure. Here we can be held and perhaps know, perhaps remember. I feel this whenever I am swimming in a Northern Ontario lake, or paddle boarding on a watery channel that snakes through an Ottawa suburb, or recalling the tumultuous waves of the Caribbean sea of my childhood. I feel that the water carries all the creatures that have ever swum, lived, and died within it. I sometimes wonder if we are only vessels. The water rides from place to place, like an entity, as we drink it in and piss it out in another land — ensuring that the larger body of its own existence continues. Because the sea is the sea, is the lake, is the stream, is the body, is the ocean. The waves live within us. Sometimes, I think we might just be the watery arms of this extended being, powerful, wild, and unwieldy, that remembers itself relentlessly.

•

That concert at Massey Hall, in my sky seat above the stage where a stranger fed me mints a long time ago, has resurfaced throughout my life. It is here again, in my sphere of memory for further integration. It reminds me that I have been repeatedly saved. Am I talking of god, of spirit? Of Thai forest monks or a shaman from Burkina Faso, a priestess or Iemanjá the goddess of the sea, or my own efforts at expansion? A bit of this, a bit of that. I think I am saved over and over again, not by one thing but by multitudes. Some oceanic strength forces me to love differently, or to take down and rebuild some shadowy aspect of self.

Today, anyone I meet from Cabo Verde tells me Cesária Évora is their cousin. I realize they may not mean precisely in terms of family lineage. Cabo Verde is a small country with shared lives and histories, and family can be more than bloodlines. So, with that thought in mind, I propose that we be cousins. And just for now, come sit with me in weakness and tears, fear and remembering, in joy and sodade. Come sit with me. You, me, and Cesária. For a moment we rise in her undulating voice. We do not drown. We listen — heads held gently above water.

# Joy

Quarter-inch-wide strips of elastic sewn onto soft pink fabric by our mothers held our ballet slippers onto our feet. We wore "flesh tone" tights on our little brown legs. My parents spoke of dancers Beryl McBurnie and Geoffrey Holder. They openly admired writers like CLR James and Derek Walcott. I don't think, however, that they expected me to take their unspoken messages about the importance of such things quite so seriously, resulting in me becoming a poet with a propensity for dancing.

I proceeded to study science at university, as expected. There I dabbled in ballet and African dance clubs. I then drifted from dance and did not enter a studio again until decades later — this time, with a sense of urgency. At that point, my hands were hurting from playing percussion in an escola de samba. I was disoriented, post-divorce, frightened, and worn out by the relentless search for emotional safety and material survival. The band had performed often with samba dancers. The dancers looked fabulous in their feathers, eyelash extensions, glitter, and heels. They moved powerfully and sensually through space. I need some of that, I thought. I laid down my drumsticks and found myself a dance class.

Samba was taught by an Italian Canadian who'd studied herself out of ballet and into considerable expertise in Afro-Brazilian dance. "Women in the North cannot move their hips," she said. I'm from the Caribbean, I've got this, I thought. I looked in the dance studio mirror and saw stiffness as I moved my own ample hips side to side. I did not have it. Years of ballet had not prepared me well. She told us that we were all beauties, that we were goddesses. She said that our bodies were luscious and glorious.

"Your hips are to be shaken. If the flesh on your thighs is not jiggling, it's not samba!" she yelled.

I learned about the origins of samba in the Afro-Brazilian religion of Candomblé. When I danced the Orixá Iemanjá, I became the goddess of the sea, mother, protector, and was fluid and sensual, with the infinite power of the waves. When I danced Xangô, the male god of justice, I threw bolts of lightning at the sky. I was fiery, direct, and clear in my intentions. As Oxumarê the snake, I slithered through the grass. My right hand was the head and I used it to bite and stop someone in their tracks, while my left arm, the snake's tail, swung around to point to and indicate a better way to live. I was Ossaim, the medicine man who drank too much. I stumbled around and yet made brilliant medicines out of plants from the forest. In these movements we explored how to be one thing and yet another — fierce and generous, resilient and wild, to hold a multitude of possibilities, a multiplicity of selves. Perhaps the movement vocabulary of Afro-Brazilian dance, of samba, could inform a new way for me to live.

The weekly gathering of women always began with flourishes of supportive hugs, kisses, and compliments. As my joints and muscles became supple, I learned to move joyously, taking up space in my worlds. I was re-energized, rediscovering resilience, balance, and sensuality. I never did wear the feathers and heels, but I learned to move through the world as if I was powerfully, playfully, sensually wearing them.

•

And then one day, I did. I put them on. All of them — the shiny red body-fitting suit, the heels, the makeup. I'd called in and paid for a photographer and studio, hired a makeup artist, rented the costume, and invited my dance instructor to attend and guide me as I sought to create an hour-long ritual for myself — part hubris, part ceremony, part experiment, part celebration. With the process of adornment, I was expanding my expression of self. The passista makeup artist stuck eyelashes on my lids. The glue made my eyes water and turn a leaky red. My thighs felt exposed and wobbly. I put my feet into the six-inch platform heels and stood awkwardly and wondered, How does anyone dance in these?

What I had in mind was a coming together of many things. In a series of photos, I hoped to capture my love of this form of movement, a moment of flourishing, a victory through all that would shut me in.

Finally, the bejewelled crown was placed on my head. The red feathers blossomed four feet into the air, leaping like thoughts, ideas, and confirmations.

•

In *The Dragon Can't Dance*, novelist Earl Lovelace describes the experience of being on the inside of a Carnival costume. One becomes one with it, holding oneself in "that important calm of the masquerader who parades before the judges, filled with the sense of the character he portrays." As I looked out from inside of the mask-like samba dancer makeup, I recalled a childhood experience. It was 1970. My father had arranged for my younger brother, Carlos, and I to have individual costumes made for us by Gerry DeFreitas for the Carnival band Africa, Africa. On the day of the Kiddies Carnival competition, I'd crawled under the sequined flap to stand inside my big mas', African Goddess of Fertility. I'd chipped my way to centre stage. Then as I turned to face the judges, something within me shifted. I raised myself to my full height, lifting the entire weight of the costume on my small shoulders, and started to dance. A mask can allow for transformation, a kind of liberation, and for a few glorious minutes, me and the Goddess, the Goddess, me, shook ourself from side to side. We rocked, we spun, and I, the African Goddess of Fertility, held court, witnessed by the crowd, the judges, and the ancestors. After dancing the costume to the end of the stage, I walked it down the ramp and crawled out from inside of it. I shifted back into my usual self, smiling shyly at the ground. My father was standing close by. He laughed, eyebrows raised, and then roared proudly with a kind of awe, "What was that?!"

Now, dressed as a passista, I was experiencing something similar. We are taught as girls and women to restrict ourselves, to rein ourselves in to live in small, tight places. As a child in my Carnival costume, the extensions of cockiyea had extended my being six feet in all directions. When swaying my body, I'd felt the strands to be wings, waves, writing on the sky. In the photography studio, as an adult woman, my arms reach outward, fingertips seeking to touch the ether. And in the mask of makeup and a blood-red costume, I felt myself carrying some essence of Iansã whose colours I wore. It is she who brushes away all bad things and brings in the good. Her red clothing represents vibrancy, blood, power, death, birth.

The photographer showed me the shots he'd taken to check angles and see if his work matched my vision. I referred to the image before me as "she," meaning the entity I was embodying. The one who came through fire to be here.

·

The opposite of motion is to freeze. The third of the conventionally accepted responses to trauma. Although I hear that "fawn" and "fit in" have now been added to the triptych of fight, flight, or freeze. These are the myriad of minute and rapid calculations below the level of consciousness that inform the being of the safest way to respond to a physical, psychological, or psychic threat. A deer may freeze in response to a hunter or a car in its path. Freezing was also my bodily response to myriad tiny yet relentless insults to the psyche. Some blows have been overt, predictable even.

Told by a boss, no, I don't see you in that position.

Told by a lawyer, you do not deserve justice.

Told by a doctor, leave, I will not treat your pain.

I've often just continued my work, as I was in a vulnerable position or had a more important task to get to or I just did not have time to teach someone how to behave. Sometimes, I can't believe that it's happening again, today, still. The hostilities, slights, aggressions, covert jibes, omissions, and scenarios where when I attempt to right myself, a white person or their representative gets upset or dangerous at being rejected, challenged, or just told to stop. And sometimes I freeze. It looks like carrying on. It is continuing to put one foot in front of the other, to get on the bus each morning and travel across town to an office, sit at a desk, and do a job that I'm grossly overqualified for, without energy to do differently, to find a different job perhaps, as I'm perpetually exhausted by the knowledge that the real decisions are made back of house and that my education or experience is not relevant.

A recent decision against the Canadian Human Rights Commission confirmed that the organization was systemically oppressing its Black employees. I felt my work experiences validated. I landed well — eventually. There is still, however, the issue of missing pay for years of lateral moves and underpromotion.

During these and various other hindrances, however, I've always had workarounds. Among the myriad of minute and rapid calculations made to stay safe in hostile environments, I learned to be in motion while appearing to be still. As a child, I felt myself as if on an observation perch, watching people and the external worlds carefully. Alien-like, I felt apart from most goings-on and watched from within myself. This method developed in childhood, became fine-tuned as an adult.

While outwardly safe and still, immobilized by expectations, respectability, or psychic blows, I could run in my thoughts, flee with my racing ideas. This dissociation or dislocation, which I will also call a capacity, was once caught by a theatre teacher, expert acting instructor David Smukler. I had travelled to Burnaby, British Columbia, to partake in the National Voice Intensive, a workshop for performers. Here my ability was pulled into a conscious vocabulary. Two acting instructors watched me disappear behind my eyes. Smukler said to his colleague, "Watch her eyes. Watch. Watch. There. She's gone. See it? She disappears. Unbelievable."

I guess that's a skill — hiding in plain sight. Another kind of magic.

•

In the quest for emotional safety, first you must know that you are at risk. If you are frozen, you can forgo knowing risk, as the fear remains unnamed. I was Canadian-born but raised during my early years in the Caribbean. Upon return to Canada, I lived an immigrant experience without the language to name it. I was technically a citizen, but without any connection to this land. Traumas can be small, daily, repeated "licks" of a new environment. I might have done well to go through immigrant supports for some kind of recalibration to this new reality. Traumas can also be unnamed, drifting, ancestral memory. Even now, I can still freeze and retreat, only moving secretly behind the eyes.

Barbara Browning is both a writer and a dancer. In her book *Samba: Resistance in Motion*, she writes specifically of Afro-Brazilian dance, including the origins and practices of samba and Orixá dance movement. She writes of "corporeal intelligence"[1] the idea that dance carries story and meaning. So many tales embodied and carried over the Atlantic Ocean in kidnapped Africans. Histories in a gesture. Relief in repeated rhythmic footsteps.

In 2020, a strange imposition made many of our worlds stand still. My body recognized a better option to its habitual freeze response. I understood that to stay clear, I must move, and so I walked for hours. And during a short window of time, when the dance studios were open, I danced. When the studios closed again, I understood something to be true: you must dare to dance. And on a dark night, in the empty parking lots of a locked-down city, or under a spotlight in a deserted schoolyard, I danced. I practised salsa steps with a man who would become my beloved because, among other things, he put a phone in his pocket with the volume turned up loud so that we could dance in winter boots on stony ground. Resistance looks like dancing in the dark on isolated streets under softly falling snow. Resistance is motion. We danced even when all around us was still.

A movement from behind the eyes is a kind of dance, is it not? My mother experiences licks as she grows old and her body does not move as she wishes it to. She resists. She taps one finger on the plastic table at her retirement home and for a moment is lost in the motion and the music. I recall my father before he died, holding a clave that I'd given him for his ninetieth birthday, gently tapping the wooden pieces together — a few seconds of weary pleasure.

Today, I am at the National Ballet School in Toronto for a dance workshop. I have come full circle. I've shown up in comfortable black dancewear. I wear black runners — no pink ballet slippers, no sparkly red onesie, no masking of any kind. I bring what my body remembers, every step, every gesture I've made up until this very point. Movement, says a former teacher of mine, philosopher and dancer Rosangela Silvestre, activates "deep human memory."[2] It can be what Browning refers to as "narrative compression into lyrical movement."[3]

Today's workshop, Afro Caribbean Journeys in Dance, is led by Lua Shayenne and Esie Mensah. I lean forward, assuming the posture that Lua demonstrates for what is my first movement to a rhythm from the Malinke culture. It is very different from samba's upright posture and swivelling hips. I am excited, pumped, joyful. My neural networks are ready. What will I be remembering? What stories will come forth?

# The Year of Jazz

*This essay takes the form of a jazz standard. Nestled within the intro and outro are alternating A and B sections. I am sustained by John Coltrane's music and the company of a dog named Jazz, as I liken the experience of lockdown to that of a bizarrely acquired concussion.*

## Intro

The alpha puppy, I learn later, is untrainable. Determined. Feisty. Smart. Bossy. Mischievous. An improviser. Will not fetch. The dog trainer gave her back after a week of residential training. He never cashed my cheque.

My child and I named her Jazz. Life is complex. The child says, Jazz, short for Jasmine. I say, The puppy's name was Coltrane's fault as she was to become one of "My Favorite Things." His version of the eternal tune. Precious and unfathomable.

# A

When the tent pole first went up my nose, it shook up my brain and me so much that I took a bit of a break and went off to Bermuda — or was it Brazil? I had not travelled to Brazil yet at that time, so it must have been Bermuda. A place I've never been drawn to and never wished to go.

I pulled the tent pole from my left nostril. Blood gushed out onto the sands of Sunnyside Beach. I turned quickly away so that my child and the other kids would not see. My friend Jacqueline gathered them and pulled them far away. I moved north-ish. A stranger sat me down on a bench. She called an ambulance. The attendants asked a few questions. They smothered laughs. A tent pole up the nose? An ambulance for a nosebleed? It was a two-minute drive to the hospital.

An emergency room doctor said, "Take a couple of days off of work" and wrote a note to that effect. On day two at home, however, the world seemed too bright, the sidewalk would not stay still. No one else was squinting at the too-bright sun. No one else swayed. Their sidewalks appeared to be stable. Perhaps it was me. I went back inside, put on my shades, and made my way gingerly to a walk-in medical clinic. I removed my shades, the doctor looked briefly into my eyes. "Go back to the hospital immediately. This is for an emergency CAT scan," he said, handing me a slip of paper.

An hour or three later, the procedure was completed and a white man in hospital scrubs raced into the examining room waving a grey scan. "Nothing obvious," he told me, "but stay at home for two weeks and follow up with your general practitioner."

I returned home, the sidewalk tipping generously from left to right, the sun a distant, piercing, bright light. I called my brothers, they laughed. I laughed. It sounded ridiculous. Tent pole up my nose.

# A

Date of Injury (DOI): March 19.

"Post-concussional type syndrome resulting from a very focal injury," wrote Scott McCullagh, MD, neuropsychiatrist. Brain Injury Clinic at Sunnybrook Hospital. He'd never seen such an injury. A blow to the inside of the head.

"It is called 'mild,'" he said apologetically, knowing full well the catastrophic impact it was having on my life. I was suddenly disabled and could not work. I slept a lot. I went for short walks. I made simple meals for my child and me. I swept the floor. I went to appointments.

Eventually, the thought arose, perhaps from my gut, that this might be an appropriate time to get a puppy. My child had been asking for one for a year, or was it two? I was now available for the care of a baby dog. It would sleep a lot. It would need very short walks. Just like me. I would be home when it needed to pee hourly. My child, now eleven, was also old enough to participate in dog care.

Two months after the DOI, on May 9, I brought Jazz home.

# B

On that day in March, on a city beach, we had been trying to create a paradise for the children. Two women dreaming of a camp-out with tents and books and games. We'd imagined the children snuggled in the tent, with sand and cool, fresh air just beyond the *seuil*.

Jacqueline and I had bonded on the sidewalk in front of Lansdowne Public School, where we waited for the buses that would take our kids to schools in other neighborhoods. Despite our vastly different economic positions — she owned multiple houses;

I owned not much — we shared, among other things, Caribbean parentage and a deep wound. The educational systems in our respective homelands, hers England, mine Canada, had ignored two little Black girls, seeing us in one dimension and relegating us to invisibility, our giftedness unnoticed. Our folks, schooled in the Caribbean, had left the advocacy for our best interests to the teachers, as was common there. They were busy navigating their new work worlds. My nurse-midwife mother, trained in natural childbirth in the Caribbean, had been told, among other things, "our women don't give birth like that."

We'd invented weekly Mastery Meetings, where we'd list what we'd accomplished personally, how we'd developed as people, the challenges that we'd vanquished, the smiles that we'd maintained, the courage that we'd exhibited, the tears and the tears and the tears that we'd shed.

Eventually, Jacqueline launched *Anancy Magazine*, an online publication that highlighted Black artists. She provided me with carte blanche to follow my interests. I wrote about music and dance and other elements of culture and spirituality.

We continued to meet and list what else we wanted to create. I was looking for Stillness. I wanted the struggles to stop. The racing. The demands on my being that were relentless. I wanted the blows to go away and allow me to — just — be — quiet. And so they did. Perhaps the spirits took control. Be careful what you ask for. Be specific.

## A

My mother sat on the red couch nestled between two dark wood end tables. She'd flown in to check up on her concussed daughter. She was in nurse mode, observing me carefully while trying to hide her concern. My child and I stood with our backs to the stone wall in the living room, each holding a violin. One of us took a sharp sip of breath at the "and" after the fourth beat and we began. The Suzuki system requires that a parent also learn the instrument to accompany, inspire, and encourage the child, and I'd bought myself a mid-level Czech violin and enthusiastically learned along with them. That night, we played a gavotte for my mother. Then I played a solo. Then my child soloed. We did two more duets.

I made no mistakes that night. I played with a joy, ease, and precision that I'd never experienced before or since.

Oliver Sacks wrote in *Musicophilia: Tales of Music and the Brain* that brain injuries can remove inhibition. Whatever limiting habits we carry in our thoughts and beliefs can be lifted when the brain stops its usual patterns. We can become *dis*inhibited. And something pure and wonderful has an opportunity to flow through us. My savant moment lasted about twenty-six minutes.

# B

Jazz was a little savant herself. We'd trained her to bat a bell hung at the front door with her paw to tell us she wanted to go out. As my child ran to open the door, Jazz ran in the other direction and threw herself onto a coveted spot, the blue beanbag chair. She made us laugh.

In *Doctor Dogs: How Our Best Friends Are Becoming Our Best Medicine*, Maria Goodavage explains how dogs can be trained to predict a migraine or a drop in blood glucose levels in the microseconds before these events come to human awareness. They are particularly effective in helping regulate our emotions. Experiencing supreme love can decrease anxiety and increase quality of life. I learned this during the year of concussion, the first year of Jazz's life. The two of us walked for as long as my brain could handle the complex work of moving through space and time. She sported a bright-red leash, and I, an invisible injury and sunglasses that highlighted my sun-infused brownness and facial structure. We strolled through the late spring mornings and afternoons for minutes at a time. Each venture was followed by hours of rest for us both.

## A

Years later, Jazz once again provided what might formally be called animal-assisted therapy or animal-assisted interventions. During lockdown, her existence gave me a reason to wander through the deserted Toronto streets. It was my duty to keep her exercised and allow her to relieve herself. As I cared for her, I cared for myself — walking for hours through the distress of a shattered relationship, a dying father, isolation, and the daily trauma of Blackness in North America.

In social isolation, I wrote only while accompanied by Coltrane. The music held me in its boundless, firm, and nebulous structure as I dug into that which is not knowable, better at times forgotten and yet so integral to one's path, that it lingered, hovered, shimmering just above my head. I was held in Coltrane's leaps and hovers. As the outside world shuddered and stumbled, I lived inside his Classic Quartet.

"John Coltrane's sound rearranges molecular structure," said Carlos Santana in the documentary *Chasing Trane*. That explains it, I think. The album was my external path to disinhibition. It was a better route than a blow to the head. It allowed the ghosts to come forth. An imposed quiet of a brain injury held me then. The imposed stillness of this time is familiar. The streets are empty and yet, this time, I am not alone in my distress. This time, the world is with me. Everyone's sidewalk tilts.

## A+

A shaman said that the blow to the left side of my being had been a blow to the sacred feminine. A deep wound that is now healing. "I've found you've got to look back at the old things and see them in a new light," said Coltrane. I think he lived somewhere ecumenical and beyond labels and scriptures. Perhaps he would have understood.

I was lucky. I recovered from the concussion. Well, there are a few behavioural vestiges. I give over to the invisible. To intuition. To spirit. I move fast, knowing for sure that it is okay to be gone before the incident begins. I change my mind. I drop in a French word in conversation. Right word. Wrong language. I am sensitive to light and will continue to read even as evening falls, until I am comfortably wrapped in darkness. Like my dog, who changes direction abruptly to pull me home, long before I've consciously decided to do so, I'm left with the ability to discern the unspoken, any subtext, and most bullshit.

## Outro

Today we walk the silent streets. Jazz is deliriously happy to be outdoors. We cross the road to avoid the droplets of breath in a jogger's slipstream. Sirens careen around us. I hold the red leash. She pulls suddenly to throw herself enthusiastically onto a patch of grass that holds molecules of shit and urine left by others of her kind. She still does not fetch.

We walk to the spot of sand on Sunnyside Beach where I was injured years ago. It is 7:30 a.m., before the hordes of sunseekers and quarantine-avoiders arise. There is now a groomed and fenced butterfly garden at the site. "No dogs beyond the fence," says a sign. There are warnings encouraging all to stay the distance of three geese apart. And oh! A paddleboarder drifts by — and another. Jazz sees them first. She is not held up in thought. She lives in disinhibition. She is my teacher at times. And sometimes I remember the lesson.

The world is rewiring itself. It is revealing the interstitial spaces between each atomic note.

Jazz is with me still. Coltrane has my back.

# Acknowledgements

've been writing for some time; however, it took a while to get to this particular spot of producing my first collection of essays in book form with a traditional publisher. I'd like to thank anyone who has inspired, encouraged, or paid me at any point along the way. I am particularly indebted to an editor who once killed a journalism story. Through a series of coincidences, this led directly to my studying at the King's University MFA program, nestled within the Department of Journalism. A subsequent collaboration with mentor Gillian Turnbull on an article for *The Conversation* was an important stepping stone in introducing my music and culture writing to a wider audience. My work with the Draft Reading Series and founder Maria Meindl introduced me to a deeper literary citizenship, where I've thrived doing readings, hosting, and curating the 2023 season, *Mixed Tongues*. I was also commissioned by Draft to create a new work, and recorded my poem "A Devotional Quartet" with the great jazz saxophonist Michael Arthurs.

Thanks so much to the folks at Dundurn Press, in particular Kwame Scott Fraser who reached out to me and opened the door for this book to flourish. When I first met Alison Isaac, I realized that she already knew my work from the *Humber Literary Review*. With these important initial meetings with Kwame and Alison, I knew that my voice was understood and embraced. Alison later edited the collection. With her wide cultural literacy, she has been the ideal person for me to work with.

Thanks to all of my initial readers, including the other two members of my lovely writing trio, Elida Schogt and Suzanne Elki Yoko Hartmann. Readers Leon Raphael Liberman, Damarise Ste Marie, and my MFA mentor group — I appreciate your insights.

Music is a part everything that I write. For that, I thank all of my major musical influences. This includes my many guitar teachers, fellow songwriters at Fat Albert's Coffee House, members of the various iterations of my band, and my time in Toronto's baterias learning to play agogô and tamborim. My dance instructors in Trinidad, Canada, and Brazil — every single one of you — I am grateful for your teachings and your dedication to your art. Music and dance have always have informed, sustained, and delighted me.

Thanks to my friend and fellow traveller Jacqueline L. Scott, my brilliant brothers, Carlos and Roberto, and my child, Z, for whose presence I am deeply grateful. The greatest thanks are for my mother, Merle, who inspired and confirmed my love of language, and my father, Stephen, who filled our home with music and books, even as they both counselled me not to go into that stuff. The environment they created ensured that, with my sensibilities, I would do just that.

# Publication History

Excerpts from this collection were previously published in whole or in part in the following publications:

"Passage" appeared in the *Malahat Review*, was awarded the Open Season Awards Creative Nonfiction Prize, 2023, and has been nominated in the Personal Journalism category for the 47th National Magazine Awards, 2024.

"The Year of Jazz" appeared in *World Literature Today* and was nominated for the Pushcart Prize, 2022.

"Ghost" was shortlisted for the Queen Mary Wasafiri New Writing Prize in 2022, and a first version was published on wasafiri.org, June 2023.

"Black Cake Buddhism" appeared in the *Humber Literary Review*.

An excerpt from "Joy" appeared in *THIS Magazine*.

Excerpts from "Music Notes" appeared in *Medium* and on cbc.ca.

Excerpts from "Water" appeared in the *Globe and Mail*.

"Hummingbird" is part of an anthology from Brindle and Glass, an imprint of TouchWood Editions.

# Notes

## GHOST

1   Selwyn Ryan, *Eric Williams: The Myth and the Man* (Saint Andrew Parish: University of the West Indies Press, 2009), 652.

## THE YELLOW DRESS

1   Duncan McLaren, *Looking for Enid: The Mysterious and Inventive Life of Enid Blyton* (London: Granta U.K., 2008), 10.
2   Gerard Besson, "T&T Folklore Pt. 4: La Diablesse," Trinbago Stories, May 2018, youtube.com/watch?v=vnHVbpDdbZI.

## HUMMINGBIRD

1   Alexxa Gotthardt, "How to Be an Artist, According to Georgia O'Keeffe," Artsy, March 11, 2018, artsy.net/article/artsy-editorial -artist-georgia-okeeffe.

## ANCESTOR

1   Arnold Thomas, "Adaptation and Survival in a Small Society: The Indians of St. Vincent and the Grenadines," *Global Indian Diaspora: Charting New Frontiers* 2 (November 2021): doi.org /10.4324/9781003246091.

2   Paul Crooks, *A Tree Without Roots: The Guide to Tracing British, African and Asian Caribbean Ancestry* (United Kingdom: Arcadia Books Ltd., 2008), 102.

3   Ibid., 101.

4   Ibid., 104.

## TRAINS AND LAUNDROMATS

1   Diedre Mask, *The Address Book: What Street Addresses Reveal About Identity, Race, Wealth, and Power* (New York City: St. Martin's Press, 2020), 183.

2   Pablo Neruda, *Residence on Earth* (New York City: New Directions Books, 1973), 241.

3   Debra Thompson, *The Long Road Home: On Blackness and Belonging* (Toronto: Simon & Schuster, 2022), 15.

## THE MATHEMATICS OF RAGE

1   Aminatta Forna, *The Window Seat: Notes from a Life in Motion* (New York City: Grove Press, 2021), 192–93.

2   Idil Abdillahi, *Black Women Under State: Surveillance, Poverty, & the Violence of Social Assistance* (Winnipeg: ARP Books, 2022), 10.

## MUSIC NOTES

Lyrics from Sam Larkin's "Sally On" from the album *The Secret Songs of Sam Larkin*, produced by Bob Wiseman.

Lyrics from my song "Seven Secrets" from the album *Seven Secrets*, produced by Rob Poizner and Bob Wiseman.

## TRIFECTA

1 Lorna Goodison, "New Year's Morning 1965," in *Mother Muse* (Montreal: Véhicule Press, 2022), 13.

2 "King's & Slavery: A Scholarly Inquiry" (December 2017): 1, ukings.ca /administration/public-documents/slavery-scholarly-inquiry.

3 Ibid.

4 Dr. Afua Cooper, et al., "Report on Lord Dalhousie's History on Slavery and Race, Executive Summary" (September 2019): 10, cdn.dal.ca /content/dam/dalhousie/pdf/dept/ldp/Lord%20Dal%20Panel %20Final%20Report_web.pdf.

5 Deanne Aline Marie Leblanc, "The Roles of Settler Canadians within Decolonization: Re-evaluating Invitation, Belonging and Rights," *Canadian Journal of Political Science/Revue canadienne de science politique* 54, no. 2 (2021): 356–73. doi.org/10.1017 /S0008423920001274. I'd never seen the term "arrivant" before and as I always felt unsure about the term settler as it applied to my history, I included it. The artists and academics that follow have dug more deeply into this concept: "In juxtaposition to the settler is the arrivant — a term initially identified in the work of Caribbean poet Kamau Brathwaite and borrowed by Jodi Byrd. This term refers to 'those people forced into the Americas through the violence of European and Anglo-American colonialism and imperialism around the globe.'" [Jodi Byrd, *Transit of Empire: Indigenous Critiques of Colonialism* (Minneapolis, University of Minnesota Press, 2011).] While the term is principally used to identify the role of slaves and indentured servants within the literature, it could also be extended to women like the *filles du roi*, who were (in many cases) forced to come to New France to settle and help populate the French-Canadian colonies. [Hubert Charbonneau, et al., *The First French Canadians: Pioneers in the St. Lawrence Valley* (Cranbury: Associated University Presses, 1993).] This term is used to identify involuntary colonists who experience(d) subordinate roles of domination within the colonial project and yet who may still be implicated as colonists. Such colonists can be either temporary or permanent.

6   "President's Commission on Slavery and the University," Universities Studying Slavery (University of Virginia): slavery.virginia.edu /universities-studying-slavery/.

7   Craig Steven Wilder, *Ebony and Ivy: Race, Slavery, and the Troubled History of America's Universities* (New York City: Bloomsbury Publishing, 2013), 1.

8   Ibid., 33.

9   Cooper, "Dalhousie's," 21–22.

10  Afua Cooper, "Negro Cemeteries," in *Copper Woman and Other Poems* (Toronto: Natural Heritage Press, 2006), 25.

11  Cooper, "Dalhousie's," 6.

12  Ibid.

13  Lawrence Hill, *The Book of Negroes* (Toronto: Harper Collins, 2011), 6.

14  Cooper, "Dalhousie's," 21.

15  Shirley Tillotson, "How (and How Much) King's College Benefited from Slavery in the West Indies, 1789 to 1854" (May 6, 2019): 15, ukings.ca/wp-content/uploads/2019/07 /TillotsonKingsAndSlaveryIndirectConnectionsMay6.pdf.

16  Cooper, "Dalhousie's," 7.

17  Morgan Mullin, "Halifax Hosted Slavers' Ships. Now It Is Home to Canada's First Institute of Slavery Studies," *Coast*, April 5, 2021.

18  Afua Hirsch, "Universities Must Follow Glasgow and Own Up to Their Role in the Slave Trade," *Guardian*, September 18, 2018, theguardian.com /commentisfree/2018/sep/18/universities-glasgow-slavery-pasts-legacy.

19  Ibid.

## JOY

1   Barbara Browning, *Samba: Resistance in Motion* (Bloomington: Indiana University Press, 1995): xi.

2   Gloria Blizzard, "Rosangela Silvestre and Deep Human Memory: In a Forest Studio in Brazil Open to the Elements," *Dance International* 46, no 4 (Winter 2018): 23.

3   Browning, *Samba*, xxiii.

# Bibliography

Abdillahi, Idil. *Black Women Under State: Surveillance, Poverty, & the Violence of Social Assistance*. Winnipeg: ARP Books, 2022.

Besson, Gerard. "T&T Folklore Pt. 4: La Diablesse." *Trinbago Stories*. May 6, 2018. youtube.com/watch?v=vnHVbpDdbZI.

Blizzard, Gloria. "Rosangela Silvestre and Deep Human Memory." *Dance International* 46, no 4 (Winter 2018): 23.

Browning, Barbara. *Samba: Resistance in Motion*. Bloomington: Indiana University Press, 1995.

Cooper, Afua, "Negro Cemeteries," in *Copper Woman and Other Poems*. Toronto: Natural Heritage Press, 2006, 25.

Cooper, Afua, et al. "Report on Lord Dalhousie's History on Slavery and Race." Dalhousie University website. September 2019. cdn.dal.ca /content/dam/dalhousie/pdf/dept/ldp/Lord%20Dal%20Panel %20Final%20Report_web.pdf.

Crooks, Paul. *A Tree Without Roots: The Guide to Tracing British, African and Asian Caribbean Ancestry*. United Kingdom: Arcadia Books Ltd., 2008.

Forna, Aminatta. *The Window Seat: Notes from a Life in Motion*. New York: Grove Press, 2021.

Goodison, Lorna. "New Year's Morning 1965," in *Mother Muse*. Monteal: Véhicule Press, 2022.

Gotthardt, Alexxa. "How to Be an Artist, According to Georgia O'Keeffe." Artsty (March 11, 2018): artsy.net/article/artsy-editorial-artist -georgia-okeeffe.

Hill, Lawrence. *The Book of Negroes*. Toronto: Harper Collins, 2011.

Hirsch, Afua. "Universities Must Follow Glasgow and Own Up to Their Role in the Slave Trade." *Guardian*, September 18, 2018. theguardian.com /commentisfree/2018/sep/18/universities-glasgow-slavery-pasts -legacy.

Leblanc, Deanne Aline Marie. "The Roles of Settler Canadians within Decolonization: Re-evaluating Invitation, Belonging and Rights." *Canadian Journal of Political Science/Revue canadienne de science politique* 54, no. 2 (2021): 356–73. doi.org/10.1017 /S0008423920001274.

Mask, Diedre. *The Address Book: What Street Addresses Reveal About Identity, Race, Wealth, and Power*. New York City: St. Martin's Press, 2020.

McLaren, Duncan. *Looking for Enid: The Mysterious and Inventive Life of Enid Blyton*. London: Granta UK, 2008.

Mullin, Morgan. "Halifax Hosted Slavers' Ships. Now It Is Home to Canada's First Institute of Slavery Studies." *Coast*, April 5, 2021.

Neruda, Pablo. *Residence on Earth*. New York City: New Directions Books, 1973.

Ng, Nathan. Station Fixation. stationfixation.com/p/alphabetical-station -selector.html.

Ryan, Selwyn D. *Eric Williams: The Myth and the Man*. Saint Andrew Parish: University of the West Indies Press, 2009.

Thomas, Arnold. "Adaptation and Survival in a Small Society: The Indians of St. Vincent and the Grenadines." *Global Indian Diaspora: Charting New Frontiers* 2 (November 2021): doi.org/10.4324/9781003246091.

Thompson, Debra. *The Long Road Home: On Blackness and Belonging*. Toronto: Simon & Schuster, 2022.

Tillotson, Shirley. "How (and How Much) King's College Benefited from Slavery in the West Indies, 1789 to 1854."

May 6, 2019, ukings.ca/wp-content/uploads/2019/07
/TillotsonKingsAndSlaveryIndirectConnectionsMay6.pdf.

University of Virginia. "President's Commission on Slavery and the
University." Universities Studying Slavery. slavery.virginia.edu
/universities-studying-slavery.

Wilder, Craig Steven. *Ebony and Ivy: Race, Slavery, and the Troubled
History of America's Universities*. New York City: Bloomsbury Press,
2013.

# About the Author

Photo by German Prieto

Gloria Blizzard is based in Toronto, Canada. Her writing explores spaces where music, dance, spirit, race, and culture collide. She received the *Malahat Review* Creative Nonfiction Prize and has been published in *World Literature Today*, *Wasafiri*, the *Humber Literary Review*, and *Kola Magazine*. Her work has been nominated for the Pushcart Prize (2023) and the National Magazine Awards, Personal Journalism (2024). Gloria holds a Master of Fine Arts in creative non-fiction from the University of King's College. When not writing, Gloria enjoys the music of Brazil, Cuban salsa, and Coltrane. In a recent collaboration, she recorded her poem "A Devotional Quartet" with jazz saxophonist Michael Arthurs. She dances daily.